Great Buildings of
BOSTON

A Photographic Guide

by

George M. Cushing, Jr.

Text by Ross Urquhart

DOVER PUBLICATIONS, INC.
NEW YORK

Acknowledgments

This book was conceived by Anne Parker Wigglesworth, who also helped to guide it to completion. Much of the printing of photographs for this book was done by Stephen J. Kovacik. Many helpful suggestions for the text were offered by Richard Audet and Marguerite Sheffield. Most of the research for the text was done at the Massachusetts Historical Society and the Fine Arts Department of the Boston Public Library.

Photographs copyright © 1982 by George M. Cushing, Jr.
Text copyright © 1982 by Ross Urquhart.
All rights reserved under Pan American and International Copyright Conventions.

Published in Canada by General Publishing Company, Ltd., 30 Lesmill Road, Don Mills, Toronto, Ontario.
Published in the United Kingdom by Constable and Company, Ltd.

Great Buildings of Boston: A Photographic Guide is a new work, first published by Dover Publications, Inc., in 1982. Glossy prints of the photographs in this book may be ordered from George M. Cushing, Jr., 306 Newbury Street, Boston, Massachusetts 02115.

International Standard Book Number: 0-486-24219-6
Library of Congress Catalog Card Number: 81-69028

Manufactured in the United States of America
Dover Publications, Inc.
180 Varick Street
New York, N.Y. 10014

Preface

I met George Cushing in 1975 when he photographed my paintings in Boston. The next year I painted his portrait. There was hardly room in his studio for him to pose or for an easel among the cameras, lights and equipment, files, cartons, drawers and stacks of thousands of photographs. The portrait was doomed and I had to paint him again, in my studio.

From my frustration that his life's work had dominated the scene but couldn't be included in the portrait, an idea was born. I asked if I might help put his collection in order and make a book from it. With full cooperation Mr. Cushing daily brought more cartons out of storage. We looked at photographs during nine months of 1978–79 and, leaving aside all other subjects, the theme of Boston buildings emerged.

It was obvious that he is a prolific photographer and a tireless worker. I learned that his career spans 45 years and that he began his profession with art objects, interiors and architecture, and earned his major reputation in fine-arts photography. A tenth-generation New Englander, he was born and brought up in Boston, where he has spent his working life. This gives him a unique role in his medium and in his time.

Here are the results of three years' selecting, reprinting and photographing more of Boston, by a man who speaks through his camera rather than about it. The pictures are of the city he knows intimately, loves, but does not judge. His judgment is reserved for their making, and for perfecting each print as it leaves his hand.

ANNE PARKER WIGGLESWORTH

Introduction

George M. Cushing, Jr., the photographer whose work appears in this book, has a stubborn unwillingness to glorify or sentimentalize Boston with his camera, and in a city that tends to glorify itself ceaselessly and sentimentalize itself unabashedly in any case, this kind of stubborn old eye is refreshing. He does not present his subjects in dramatic poses, nor does he peer at them slyly from oblique or unusual angles. He prefers, instead, to see his subjects in their best light, and to look at them unselfconsciously in an ordinary way. For many of the buildings that were photographed for this book, the best light arrived on bright sunlit days in the early afternoon, but for others it arrived on cloudier days, and at different times: six in the morning, or even eight in the evening. Whatever the time of day, the idea was always to study the subject's unique and original qualities, and to find the best way of bringing them out in a photograph.

Mr. Cushing tends to look fairly directly at a building, in a way that the building seems to want to be looked at, but at the same time, he is not too shy to be willing to go over to his subject and have it tidy itself up a little before having its picture taken: having someone raise or lower a window shade, for example. And if there is trash on the street in front of a building, or a large truck obscuring a corner of a building, he will wait until these obstructions are cleared out of the way rather than have them distract us from his subject.

There was a similar approach used in the writing of the text: an unwillingness to sentimentalize over "the crooked and narrow streets," "the romance of old and new," or over the city's "change and continuity." While there might be something to be said for a kind of Chamber of Commerce guidebook approach—in accentuating the positive, exclusively, and in promoting the city for its own good—I would like to think that I have taken a more idealistic approach.

Arthur Gilman's observation of the art of architecture as a means of "creating sublime ideas in the mind" was itself a very sublime and useful idea, in that it rose above a concern for just the functional aspects and historical associations of buildings, and managed also to rise above the more academic preoccupation with style and influences on style. It saw the art of architecture as an abstract art, allowing for dozens of different styles, and having a civilizing effect on a city when practiced well. So with Arthur Gilman in mind, I have tried to emphasize ideas.

There is another observation that seems relevant here, and it comes from the Boston architect Clarence H. Blackall. He wrote in *Tremont Temple Sketch Book: A Description of the Edifice* [Boston, 1896]:

> It has been calculated that if it were possible for one man to do all the work incidental to the erection of this structure, assuming that the materials themselves were ready to his hand, he would be occupied for something over 350 years at his task; whereas, if he were obliged to go back to first principles, obtain all his materials from nature, fashion everything himself, more than three thousand years would elapse before he could complete his labors. These figures simply mean that in order to produce a modern structure of this nature a system of co-operation is to be put in motion which is almost as far-reaching as the ends of the world and which call into active play the agencies of thousands of men all over the country, and the enormous power of countless machines and factories.

In other words: buildings are made by people, and it is the spirit of collaboration and cooperation that gets things done. That spirit in Boston has created some of the world's finest architecture.

R. U.

Selected Bibliography

A complete bibliography is at the Massachusetts Historical Society in Boston.

Bacon, Edwin M., ed. *King's Dictionary of Boston* [Cambridge, 1883].

Boston Redevelopment Authority. *Recycled Boston* [Boston, 1976].

Boston Society of Architects. *Architecture/Boston.* Introduction by Walter Muir Whitehill. Text by Joseph L. Eldredge [Barre, Mass., 1976].

Boston Society of Architects. *Boston Architecture.* Introduction by John Coolidge [Cambridge, 1970].

Bunting, Bainbridge. *Houses of Boston's Back Bay* [Cambridge, 1967].

Bunting, W. H. *Portrait of a Port: Boston, 1852–1914* [Boston, 1971].

Chamberlain, Allen. *Beacon Hill: Its Ancient Pastures and Early Mansions* [Boston, 1955].

Damrell, Charles S. *A Half Century of Boston Building* [Boston, 1895].

Hamlin, Talbot. *Greek Revival Architecture in America* [Toronto, 1944].

Harrell, Pauline Chase, and Margaret Supplee Smith, eds. *Victorian Boston Today: Ten Walking Tours* [n.p., 1975].

Herndon, Richard. *Boston of Today* [Boston, 1892].

Hitchcock, Henry-Russell. *A Guide to Boston Architecture, 1837–1954* [New York, 1954].

Hogarth, Paul. *Walking Tours of Old Boston* [New York, 1978].

Institute of Contemporary Art, Boston. *Boston: Forty Years of Modern Architecture.* Text by William J. R. Curtis [Boston, 1980].

Kilham, Walter. *Boston After Bulfinch* [Cambridge, 1946].

McIntyre, A. McVoy. *Beacon Hill: A Walking Tour* [Boston, 1975].

Massachusetts Department of Community Affairs. *Built to Last.* Text by Gene Bunnell [Washington, D.C., 1977].

Museum of Fine Arts, Boston. *Back Bay Boston: The City as a Work of Art* [Boston, 1969].

Seaburg, Carl. *Boston Observed* [Boston, 1971].

Sweetzer, M. F. *King's How to See Boston* [Boston, 1895].

Tucci, Douglass Shand. *Built in Boston: City and Suburb, 1800–1950* [Boston, 1978].

Whitehill, Walter Muir. *Boston: A Topographical History* [Cambridge, 1968].

Great Buildings of
BOSTON

Waterfront/North End

The maritime industries in Boston prospered through the seventeenth, eighteenth and nineteenth centuries, peaking in the decades between 1830 and 1860. It would probably be an overstatement now to say that the waterfront area is being revitalized, as it may never again be as active and vital as it was during those enormously productive boom years of the last century. Still, the improvements made in the last few years have been imaginative, and are an inspiration to other cities. The changes are all the more remarkable considering the state of decline that this area experienced through much of the twentieth century up to 1970. One low point was the construction, during the 1950s, of the Central Artery, an elevated highway through downtown Boston, which isolated the waterfront and North End from the rest of the city, made the air unbreathable for North End residents, and brought about the demolition of some of the city's finest buildings. The ten-year construction plan for the Central Artery and other highways in the area was submitted to Governor Bradford in 1948 by the Joint Board for the Metropolitan Master Highway Plan. Here is an excerpt from the report: "We recommend the adoption of a modern high-speed expressway system as the foundation on which highway construction should be programmed for the ultimate solution of the problem [i.e., traffic congestion]. . . . Functional plans have been prepared for surface improvements in downtown Boston which are deemed sufficient to make possible the collection and dispersion of expressway traffic." This "ultimate solution" and its "surface improvements" were not the answer, as the city is discovering. In spite of the damage done, the waterfront and North End areas are making a comeback, with, it is hoped, a minimum of further dislocation and destruction. The photograph shows part of the waterfront and all of the skyline of Boston, from I. M. Pei's Harbor Towers on the far left to the Prudential Center on the far right. In the foreground is the Charlestown Navy Yard, established in 1800, closed down in 1974, and now run by the National Park Service. In the right background is the long granite ropewalk that was designed by Alexander Parris and built in 1834–1836.

2 WATERFRONT / NORTH END

Quincy Market, Commercial Street. Josiah Quincy was inaugurated as mayor of Boston in 1823. One of his first initiatives was to find a way to improve food distribution in the city. He and his associates proposed that the marketplace around Faneuil Hall be extended, and that a new market building be built. In 1825 the cornerstone of Faneuil Hall Market, commonly referred to as Quincy Market, was laid. The land on which the market was built was made available to the city partly by filling in the waterfront at the docks to the east of Faneuil Hall, and partly by acquiring private properties through eminent domain. When Quincy Market opened in 1826, it was met with some skepticism, but within a few years its success was an established fact, and it received general approval. The building, designed by Alexander Parris (1800–1852), is one of the finest examples of Greek Revival architecture in Boston. It is 535 feet long, 50 feet wide and two stories high, with a domed central section that is somewhat higher. The walls, of Quincy granite, are completely devoid of ornament. At either end of the building is a portico *(above)* with four columns of Chelmsford granite supporting a simple pediment. The columns are monoliths, with Doric capitals. The interior space of Quincy Market was originally divided into 128 stalls which were leased to vendors. Outside the building, in the streets running parallel to it on the north and south sides, dozens of market wagons, loaded with fruits and vegetables, would crowd the area. The two side buildings that flank Quincy Market on the north and south, called North Market and South Market, were built at the same time as the central building. Four stories high, with granite fronts, they were designed by Parris in the post-and-lintel form. By the middle of this century the three buildings, in very bad condition, were condemned for use as markets. By 1970, the Boston Redevelopment Authority had acquired the buildings and was setting in motion one of the country's most famous restoration projects. Quincy Market was reopened in 1976 by Mayor Kevin White; the North and South Markets in 1977. The buildings were restored by F. A. Stahl & Associates, and the new Faneuil Hall Marketplace, designed by Benjamin Thompson and developed by the James Rouse Company of Maryland, became an enormous success as a tourist attraction, with commercial enterprises occupying its stores and stalls.

Above and left: **Faneuil Hall, Faneuil Hall Square.** Peter Faneuil was born in New Rochelle, New York, in 1700. He moved to Boston around 1719, and went into business there with his uncle, Andrew Faneuil. After his uncle died, Faneuil took over the business, and in a few years was the wealthiest man in town, making his money by trading in wine, fishery products, tobacco, tar and slaves. In 1740 he proposed to build a market house at his own expense and present it to the town, centralizing the town's trading activity. The town accepted this plan, and late in the same year the construction of the building was begun. It is the only building known to have been designed by the painter John Smibert (1688–1751), who was a friend of Peter Faneuil. At some point before construction was finished in 1742, it was decided that the building should have a second story, over the market level, for use as a town meeting room. The Board of Selectmen was given offices here also, so that it could move out of the limited space available in the Old State House. Faneuil Hall, then, was the center of trade, the seat of town government, and the place where public gatherings of all kinds were held. The historical importance of the town meetings that took place here before the Revolution earned the building the name "Cradle of Liberty." In 1761, a fire

destroyed the interior of the building, but by 1763 the burnt part had been completely reconstructed. Another major reconstruction project was carried out during 1805–06, when the building was more than doubled in size. Charles Bulfinch designed this enlarged building, but his design was consistent with that of Smibert: the south wall of the original building was retained, along with part of the east and west walls. Further reconstruction was required during 1898–99, but Faneuil Hall has remained to the present day essentially as Bulfinch designed it. However, the market stalls that for more than 200 years surrounded the lower level were removed recently. This level of the building is now occupied by three snack bars and two souvenir shops. The second level is still used for public gatherings. It is exciting to think that this building has remained for so long as a historical reality, and not been packaged as a lifeless relic. The rows of round-arched windows and pilasters that run around all four sides of the building have an eternal, albeit ordinary, beauty and reflect, with their human-size proportions, a democratic spirit. One last note: atop the cupola is the original grasshopper vane (*left*) that Shem Drowne made of copper in 1742.

Above: **The Union Oyster House, 41 Union Street.** The Union Oyster House (or Capen House) is located on the Blackstone Block, at the intersection of Union and Marshall Streets. It was built ca. 1714, and its brick walls and gambrel roof, designed in the English style, make it a typical example of the houses that were built in Boston during this period. The dormer windows were probably added late in the nineteenth century. In 1742 the house was bought by Thomas Stoddard, who later bequeathed it to his daughter Patience and her husband, Hopestill Capen, who ran a dry-goods shop there until his death in 1807. His son Thomas took over the business until 1819. One of Hopestill Capen's apprentices in 1769–70 was Benjamin Thompson, later known as Count Rumford, the eminent scientist and philanthropist. Also of particular note in the building's history are the years 1771–75, during which Isaiah Thomas printed his newspaper *The Massachusetts Spy* on an upper floor. In 1826, an oyster bar, run by a man named Atwood, was established in the house. It is the ancestor of the present restaurant, which advertises itself as "the oldest restaurant in continuous service in America."

Above and left: **The Custom House, India Street at State Street.** The Custom House was designed to resemble a Greek temple, although its plan is in the form of a Greek Cross. It was built from 1837 to 1847 according to plans by architect Ammi Burnham Young (1798–1874). Around its exterior stand 32 fluted Doric columns, each of which is one solid block of Quincy granite weighing 42 tons. A Roman dome originally covered the central portion of the building, in the middle of which was a skylight 25 feet in diameter that allowed some sunlight into a central rotunda below. The Custom House cost about $1 million to build, making it one of the most expensive buildings of its time. For this and other reasons, it was controversial. One of its fiercest critics was the architect Arthur Gilman, who wrote in the *North American Review* for 1844 that "the sullen 'Caves of Domdaniel' could scarcely inspire more cheerless emotions." Of its granite masses, Gilman wrote: ". . . there is enough material for at least three buildings of the same size . . . ." Of its engaged columns ("these excrescences"): ". . . they very seriously obstruct the light of the windows, and shut in the view obtained from them to a much more confined range of vision . . . ." He termed the windows "mere holes in the wall" and the dome "its last and crowning absurdity." Of the building's cost: ". . . what idea will posterity be likely to form of the government architects of the nineteenth century, or of the government commissioners, who could abet such reckless squandering?" He questioned also "the fitness of the design to the purpose." Later critics have been kinder. The dome that Gilman criticized was removed when the present tower was added. Designed by Peabody & Stearns, it was completed in 1915.

Opposite left, above and right: **The Grain Exchange Building, 177 Milk Street.** The magnificent Grain Exchange Building, located at the intersection of India and Milk Streets, was originally the Boston Chamber of Commerce and later the Grain and Flour Exchange. It now provides space for a number of different organizations. Built in 1890–92, it was designed by the firm of Shepley, Rutan & Coolidge. The walls of the building, with their massive piers and arches in the powerful Romanesque style of H. H. Richardson, are made of a pinkish-grey granite that was quarried in Milford. The gabled conical roof (*above*) that sits crownlike on top of the front part of the building is its most striking feature.

Opposite, top: **The State Street Block.** Walter H. Kilham, in his book, *Boston After Bulfinch* [1946], described the State Street Block as "the best piece of architecture in the city." The building's walls, of rough-hammered granite that was quarried in Quincy, are an admirably solid work of construction. The granite is flint-gray, with crystals in the stone that glint in bright sunlight. The architect of the building was Gridley J. F. Bryant (1816–1899), who designed it in 1857 for the Long and Central Wharf Corporations. (The architect of hundreds of buildings in and around Boston, he may also have designed 50–52 Broad Street.) It was a massive structure then, consisting of 16 warehouses and forming an enormous line down to the water. In the 1950s, more than half of this block was demolished to make way for the Central Artery, which passes by the building now with only three or four feet to spare. Recent renovation has converted the State Street Block into a combination of shops, offices and condominiums.

Opposite, bottom: **The Mercantile Wharf Building.** At 75–117 Atlantic Avenue, this is another of the great granite blocks on the Boston waterfront, and was designed by the same architect for the Mercantile Wharf Corporation. It was built of Quincy granite in 1855–57, and was described by a journalist, writing in 1857 for *Ballou's Pictorial*, as "a leviathan structure." It, too, lay in the path of the Central Artery, and had about a third of its length demolished. In 1975, its renovation was begun by John Sharratt & Associates, who converted the building to shops and condominiums, and designed its central atrium.

Above: **Nos. 50–52 Broad Street.** The building on the corner of Milk and Broad Streets was built in 1860. A sturdy-looking structure of gray granite, it wears its mansard roof with style.

Opposite, bottom: **Commercial Wharf.** The Commercial Wharf Building, once also known as Granite Wharf, was the first of Boston's huge granite warehouses. It was built by Isaiah Rogers (1800–1869) in 1832–33 for the Commercial Wharf Corporation. When Atlantic Avenue was laid out in 1868–70 (a seven-acre landfill, using earth removed from Fort Hill), it cut through this building, destroying six of its warehouse segments and leaving two buildings where there once was one. Commercial Wharf West was renovated in 1971 by Andrew Notter Associates, in a conversion to residential and commercial use. Similar conversion to condominiums took place on Commercial Wharf (to the east of Atlantic Avenue) during 1968–69, under direction of the firm of Halasz & Halasz.

Opposite, top: **Lewis Wharf.** To the north is Lewis Wharf, which was one of Boston's earliest wharves, and was known originally as Clarke's Wharf. Later, it was called Hancock's Wharf, being the property of Thomas Hancock and then John Hancock before it acquired its present name. The Lewis Wharf Building is of granite, and was built in 1834. When Atlantic Avenue came through the area, it took away five of the warehouse segments from the building's western end. Its present state as commercial and residential space is the result of renovation work done in 1965–69 by Carl Koch & Associates.

Above: **Pilot House.** Nearby, on the same wharf, stands a brick building called the Pilot House. Built ca. 1863, it was converted in 1974 to space for offices (the upper floors) and a restaurant (first floor) by Carl Koch & Associates.

Right: **Long Wharf.** Long Wharf, or Boston Pier, as it was called originally, was laid out in 1710 by a private group of merchants, who erected a long line of brick warehouses on it. The wharf was said to be the longest on the continent, as it extended about 2000 feet out into the harbor. It has been shortened over the years, as various landfill projects on the waterfront have consumed its landward end. On the left in the photograph is the Chart House restaurant, which occupies a brick building dating from about 1830. This building, and its neighbor to the right, the Custom House Block, were renovated in 1973 by Anderson Notter Associates. The Custom House Block was built of granite in 1845 or 1846, and its design has been attributed to Isaiah Rogers. It was leased originally to the U.S. government for customs use, and is now a combination of residential space (the upper floors) and commercial space (the first floor). A large hotel will soon be built on Long Wharf, and is scheduled to open in 1982.

Below: **New England Aquarium.** Nearby, on Central Wharf, is the New England Aquarium, designed in 1969 by Cambridge Seven Associates. Central Wharf was built in 1816 and was 1240 feet long, originally, with a line of brick buildings extending along its length, providing space for 54 stores. Like Long Wharf, it has been shortened to just a fraction of its original length.

Above and opposite, top: **The Boston Fish Pier.** The Boston Fish Pier is located in South Boston, off Northern Avenue. Designed by the architect Henry F. Keyes, it serves as headquarters for the fishing industry in Boston as it has since it was built in 1912–15. Its restoration, now underway, should bring about an expanded and more efficient use of its several buildings.

Opposite, bottom: **Commonwealth Pier No. 5.** Just west of the Fish Pier is the headhouse of Commonwealth Pier No. 5, a structure in the Roman style (architect unidentified) completed in 1914. While the pier was once the largest steamship terminal in America, it now receives only an occasional freight ship or passenger cruise ship. The headhouse is used as office space by a number of organizations, and has a large exhibition hall on its third floor.

Above: **The Moses Pierce/Nathaniel Hichborn House, 29 North Square.** On November 7, 1683 the General Court of the Massachusetts Bay Colony enacted a law regarding the construction of new buildings in Boston. The law read in part: "This Court being sensible of the great Ruines in Boston by Fire, at sundry times, and hazard still of the same, by reason of the joyning and nearness of the Buildings . . . Do Order and Enact, That henceforth no Dwelling-house, Warehouse, Shop, Barn, Stable, or any other Housing, shall be Erected and set up in Boston, except of Stone, or Brick, and covered with Slate or Tyle . . . ." The brick house in the photograph was built for Moses Pierce, a glazier, in compliance with this law, ca. 1711–15. The house was designed in the English Renaissance style, its roughly symmetrical facade straining to emulate a grand manner. Moses Pierce sold the house in 1747 to William Shippard. Shippard, in turn, sold it in 1781 to Nathaniel Hichborn, a shipbuilder by occupation and a cousin of Paul Revere. The house remained in the possession of the Hichborn family until 1864, when it became a tenement, with its front area on the street level altered somewhat and used as a shop. In 1949, after a long period of neglect, the house was bought by the Moses Pierce/Williams Association. It was restored, inside and out, by Sidney and Charles R. Strickland in 1949–51. Since 1970, the house has been owned and maintained by the Paul Revere Memorial Association. This and the Revere House are probably the oldest existing structures in Boston.

Opposite: **The Paul Revere House, 19 North Square.** The house was built some time between 1676 and 1681. In its present form it is largely a reproduction of the original house, although its skeletal structure is the real thing. As reconstructed, it is a good example of the domestic architecture of its time, with its gabled roof, clapboards and casement windows with diamond panes. Standing on the site of the house of Increase Mather, the minister at the Old North Meeting House, it was built a few years after the great fire of November 27, 1676, which destroyed both the Mather house and the meeting house, as well as dozens of other buildings in the area. The house's first owner was a successful merchant named Robert Howard, who bought it in 1681. It changed hands several times during the eighteenth century, underwent some reconstruction ca. 1750–60 when a third story was probably added, and in 1770 was bought by Paul Revere. Revere and his large family lived there until 1780. Between 1780 and 1800, Revere rented it: in 1780 to George De France, and in 1784 to Joseph Dunkerly, the miniaturist. During the nineteenth century, the three-story building was a tenement, its first level being used for various commercial purposes. In 1907 the house was acquired by the Paul Revere Memorial Association. The restoration work was done in 1907–08 under the direction of Joseph Everett Chandler. The interior of the house was later furnished to reflect the style of the Colonial period. It is now open to the public as a historic-house museum.

The McLauthlin Building, 120 Fulton Street. The McLauthlin Building may date from about 1856, when William Adams & Co., safe manufacturers, moved into it. It is one of the few surviving cast-iron buildings in Boston. The design of the facade was inspired by the architecture of the Italian Renaissance: the long rows of arched windows, with thin supporting columns, the strength of which allowed the design to accommodate glass windows of unprecedented size. George T. McLauthlin was a mechanical genius who moved his machine shop there in 1861, following with his business office in 1865. For over 100 years the McLauthlin Company produced high-quality engines, water wheels, boilers, elevators and other kinds of machinery. In 1979, when the McLauthlin Company (now the McLauthlin Elevator Company) moved to Cambridge, the iron building was sold to the Fulton Street Corporation, a group of investors who made a great effort to restore the facade of the building to its original state, as well as to renovate the interior for their own purposes. The first two floors are now commercial offices, and the upper floors have been converted into condominium apartments. An additional story has been added on the top, but it is not visible from the street.

Opposite: **Christ Church (Old North Church), 193 Salem Street.** Christ Church was commonly referred to as "the North Church" in the eighteenth century, and acquired the name "Old North Church" in the nineteenth. It was made famous by the poem of Longfellow, "Paul Revere's Ride," in which the story of the beginning of the American Revolution is told. The church was founded in 1723 as a parish of the Society for the Propagation of the Gospel in Foreign Parts, a missionary society of the Church of England. It was the second Episcopal church in Boston, the first one having been King's Chapel, which had become too small to hold the growing number of Anglicans in the city. The cornerstone of the building was laid on April 15, 1723, and although the first service was held that December, the construction of the building was not completed until 1744. The architect of Christ Church has never been identified, but speculation has centered on Anthony Blount or William Price. In any case, the church was designed after those in London by Christopher Wren, or in a style that was similar to Wren's. The spire, built in 1740, was designed by William Price (1684–1771). Price, a book and print seller, a cabinetmaker and an early member of Christ Church, was also the designer of the church's first organ, serving as church organist in 1736–43. The spire that he designed was blown down and destroyed during a gale in 1804, and in 1806 a shorter one, said to have been designed by Charles Bulfinch, was built in its place. This spire lasted until 1954, when a hurricane blew it down. The present replacement was designed in 1955 by Charles R. Strickland after the original

by William Price. Its belfry holds the church's original peal of bells that were cast in 1744 and were the first bells brought to British North America. On top of the pinnacle stands the copper weathervane that Shem Drowne made for the church in 1740. It consists of a flower and pot (only part of this section remains), a ball, a banner and a five-pointed star.

Above: **St. Stephen's Church, 401 Hanover Street.** The New North Church was a Congregational religious society, founded in 1712. Its meetinghouse was built in 1714 at the corner of Hanover and Clark Streets. That building was torn down in 1804, and the present building was erected on the site in the same year. It is the only church designed by Charles Bulfinch that is still standing in Boston. The church, Unitarian in 1804, changed affiliation once again in 1862, when it was bought by the Catholic Diocese and renamed St. Stephen's Church. In 1870, when Hanover Street was widened, the building was moved 12 feet back from the street, raised up about a half-story, and set on a newly built basement. In 1870–75 the church was enlarged by an addition at the rear. During this period, the building's exterior was also altered considerably, but in 1965 it was restored to the original Bulfinch design. The restoration work was initiated by Richard Cardinal Cushing, and was carried out by Chester F. Wright. In 1968, the church's administration was turned over to the Missionary Society of St. James the Apostle, under whose care it has remained.

Beacon Hill/West End

In his book *Beacon Hill: Its Ancient Pastures and Early Mansions* [1925], Allen Chamberlain described Beacon Hill as "a little town in itself, presenting a social cross-section of the city as a whole." Several aspects of this neighborhood are illustrated in the accompanying photographs. No. 61 Beacon Street *(above)* is a picture of refinement and delicacy, with its well-proportioned design and perfect harmony of red brick, black shutters and white trim. It was built ca. 1817 for William Minot from the design of an unidentified architect. **Acorn Street** *(opposite, top)*, an antique passageway ten feet wide, is paved with cobblestones. Five of the nine houses that face this street were built by Cornelius Coolidge (1778–1843) in 1827–

29. Coolidge was an architect and building contractor who built about 50 houses on the Hill during the 1820s and 1830s. **No. 14 Walnut Street** *(opposite, bottom)* is unusual in that its entrance is at the side of the house, on the basement level. The house was built for John Callender in 1802 or 1803, and was designed by an unidentified architect. The entrance was at the front of the house originally, facing Mt. Vernon Street, but it was put at the side sometime after the grade of Walnut Street was lowered, ca. 1821, exposing the house's foundation. Ellery Sedgwick, who edited the *Atlantic Monthly* from 1908 to 1938, was one of the house's more recent occupants.

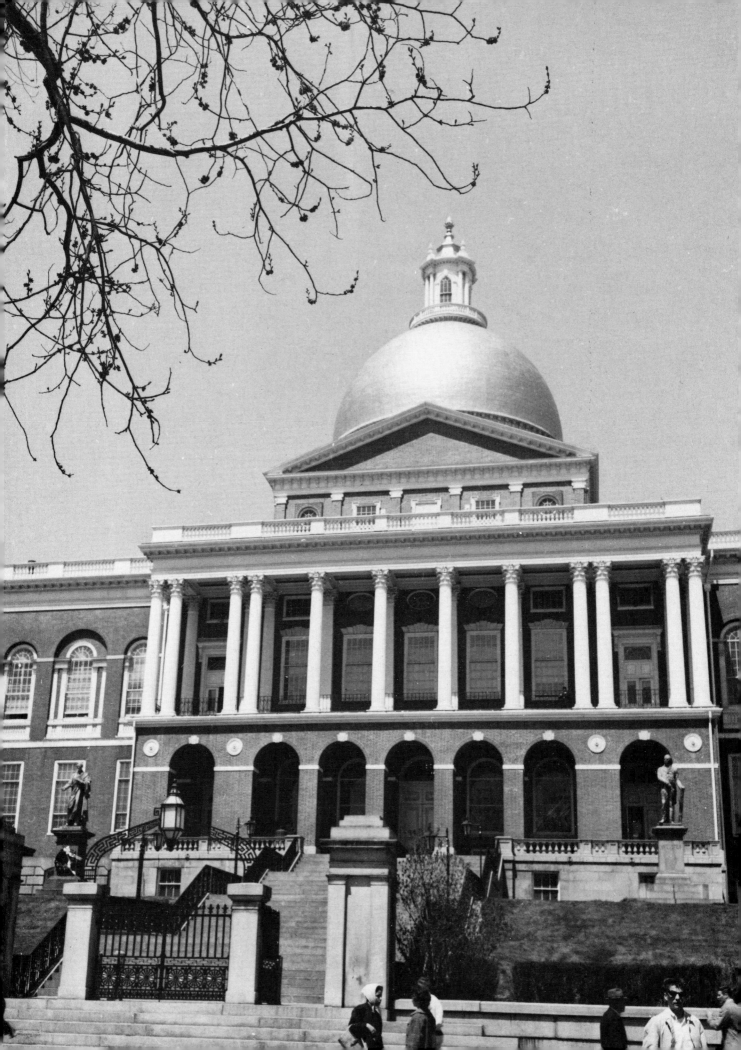

The Massachusetts State House, Beacon and Park Streets. In 1787 the Massachusetts State legislature appointed a committee to look into the possibility of constructing a new State House; that November Charles Bulfinch (1763–1844) submitted plans to this committee, offering them a design "in the style of a building celebrated all over Europe." Bulfinch, 24 years old at this time, had returned some months previously from an extensive tour on which he had observed the art and architecture of England, France and Italy. His plans for the State House were adopted in 1795, and on July 4, the building's cornerstone was laid, being dragged into position by 15 white horses. Built on the land that adjoined the mansion house of John Hancock, near the summit of Beacon Hill, the State House was perched there in grand style, one of the most widely celebrated buildings of its time. It is admired today, as it was two centuries ago, for the way that its details fit in perfect proportion with the design as a whole. The fine Palladian windows on the second story have about them an expression of intelligence and sensitivity, but are not overwhelmed by the breadth of expression in the great colonnade of white pillars or in the arches of the portico. The enormous gold dome and the lantern at the top complete the picture of unity and symmetry that the State House conveys, but neither of these qualities is so conspicuous as to seem oppressive. It is the oldest existing building on Beacon Hill, and although it appears much as it did in Bulfinch's time, there have been a number of changes. The original Corinthian columns, carved trunks of trees brought down from Maine, were removed in 1960, and reproductions of the originals, made of iron, were put in their place. The dome was covered with copper by Paul Revere in 1802, and did not receive its present gold-leaf covering until 1874. The red brick walls, painted over in yellow or white at different times in the past, were returned to their original unpainted state in 1928. In 1889–95, a large extension of the building, designed by Charles E. Brigham, was added on at the rear (*above*) and in 1914–17, the east and west wings, made of white marble and granite and designed by William Chapman, R. Clipston Sturgis and Robert D. Andrews, were added. The gates at the front were designed by Alexander Parris in 1826. Behind them, near the granite piazza, are statues of Horace Mann (by Emma Stebbins, 1865) and Daniel Webster (by Hiram Powers, 1859). The Beacon Hill monument, standing near the east side of the Brigham addition, was erected by the Bunker Hill Association in 1899. It marks the site of the original Bulfinch column, which stood at the summit of the hill before the peak was leveled to its present height.

Opposite, top: **The First Otis House, 141 Cambridge Street.** Harrison Gray Otis (1765–1848) graduated from Harvard in 1783, was admitted to the bar in 1786 and went on to become a prominent lawyer and Federalist politician. Samuel Eliot Morison, in *A Brief Account of Harrison Gray Otis*, wrote: "Endowed as he was with a winning personality, a keen intellect, the Otis gift of oratory, and numerous influential relatives, the young man quickly made his way in the world." In 1795 Otis had Charles Bulfinch design for him the mansion on the corner of Cambridge and Lynde Streets, and by the spring of 1797 the house was ready for occupancy by Otis, his wife and their four children. Its facade was austere and plain, with only the fanlights and Palladian window in the middle to hold one's attention, but it was, for its time, one of the finest houses in Boston. Otis sold the house in 1801, and in 1801 or 1802 he moved with his family to a new house on Mt. Vernon Street. The Cambridge Street house changed hands several times in the next century, its appearance deteriorating gradually as the years passed. In 1834 it was rented to a Mr. and Mrs. Williams, who ran a home for invalid men and women. Later in the century it was a rooming house, with its interior subdivided and remodeled and its exterior partly obscured in the front by a row of small shops. But in 1916 the house was bought by the Society for the Preservation of New England Antiquities, and was made into a historic-house museum, furnished in the Federal style. The Society went to considerable expense in its effort to restore the facade to its original Bulfinch design. In 1926, when Cambridge Street was widened, the Society moved the Otis house back about 40 feet, and connected it at the rear to two brick buildings on Lynde Street. More recently, a modern extension to these buildings was built, which serves as the Society's headquarters and office.

Opposite, bottom: **The Second Otis House, 85 Mt. Vernon Street.** Harrison Gray Otis was elected to Congress in 1796, but left office in 1801 because he was, as Morison explains in *A Brief Account . . . ,* "tired of his long absences from home" and "disgusted with the factional squabbles in the Federalist party." It was just before this period that Otis bought into the real-estate syndicate called the Mount Vernon Proprietors, whose ambitious plan it was to buy up all of what was then pasture land on Beacon Hill, owned by John Singleton Copley, and to develop it into an exclusive residential area. The land was bought in 1795, and within a few years most of the Mount Vernon Proprietors had built for themselves large freestanding houses on the Copley land, hoping to attract more people to the new neighborhood. Otis's new house, at 85 Mt. Vernon Street (called Olive Street until 1832), was designed ca. 1801 by Charles Bulfinch, and in either 1801 or 1802 the Otis family moved in. Now the oldest existing house on its street, the house is also one of the finest, with its solid-looking facade of brick and the genteel elegance of its pilasters on the upper stories above the row of recessed arches on the first story. Otis and his family moved out of the house in 1806, and from that year to the present it has been maintained as a private residence. Through the years it has kept much of its original appearance, the only alterations being the Greek Revival entrance on the east side (1850s) and the extension on the west side, designed in 1882 by Peabody & Stearns.

Above: **The Third Otis House, 45 Beacon Street.** Otis and family moved to their new house on Beacon Street in 1806. This one was also designed by Charles Bulfinch, Otis's lifelong friend and business associate. Otis lived in this house for over 40 years, during a period when he was U.S. senator (1816–22) and mayor of Boston (1829, 1830, 1831). It was here that he died in 1848, at the age of 83. One of the highlights in the house's history was the visit of President James Monroe to a party given by Otis in 1817. After Otis's death the house was maintained as a private residence by a succession of owners, but in 1941 it seemed headed for demolition. Fortunately, the money to save it was raised, and it was offered to the Boy Scouts of America as their headquarters. It changed hands again in 1951, when it was bought by the American Meteorological Society, under whose care the building was given extensive restoration. The Bulfinch design is straightforward and simple, apart from the grandeur of the windows on the second story, and the house is admirable in its restraint from showiness and excess.

Opposite, top: **Beacon Street.** Most of the houses that line the north side of Beacon Street as it slopes upward from Charles Street toward the State House were built during the first half of the nineteenth century. It was the view over the Common and the rest of the town that attracted the affluent to this street (once known as "the Lane to the Almshouse"), and the neighborhood reflects their taste in its architecture. Nos. 54 and 55 Beacon Street were built ca. 1807 for James Colburn, a merchant, after designs that were probably by Asher Benjamin. No. 55 was the home of the historian William Hickling Prescott in the years 1845–59, and is now a historic-house museum and headquarters of the Massachusetts branch of the National Society of the Colonial Dames of America.

Opposite, bottom: **Women's City Club.** Pictured below is another pair of twin houses: 39 and 40 Beacon Street, which have been attributed to Alexander Parris. No. 39 (on the left) was built in 1818 or 1819 for a wealthy entrepreneur named Nathan Appleton. No. 40 (on the right) was built at the same time for Appleton's friend and former business partner, Daniel Pinckney Parker. The two houses were later joined together, and are now the home of the Women's City Club. Talbot Hamlin, in *Greek Revival Architecture in America* [1944], wrote that these houses "are important because in their detail the late Colonial delicacy has almost completely disappeared and the new, firm, architectonic simplicity of the Classic Revival has taken its place." The fourth story of the building, added in 1888, was designed by the firm of Hartwell & Richardson.

Above: **70 Beacon Street.** The house of white Chelmsford granite at 70 Beacon Street, facing the Public Garden, is one of a row of six houses (70–75) built in 1828 by the Mount Vernon Proprietors on what was then newly filled-in land. Of the six houses, 70 is the one that most resembles its original appearance (the oriel window on the second story was probably added late in the nineteenth century). The architect who designed this house and its neighbors is unidentified, but the influence of Asher Benjamin has been noted in some of the details, and the style at least of the rusticated first story is English Regency. The ironwork around the large windows on this first story adds some delicacy to the effect of the whole. Overall, the house reflects a taste for simplicity and integrity.

The Somerset Club, 42 Beacon Street. Edwin M. Bacon described the Somerset Club in 1883 as "that reservoir of Boston blue blood." The building is a structure suitably dignified and imposing for the oldest and most exclusive club in Boston. It was built in 1819–22 on the site of the house of John Singleton Copley. The architect was Alexander Parris, who designed also the Quincy Market building and St. Paul's Cathedral. In its first state, as the home of David Sears, it was only two stories high, and was covered with a domed roof. The house was free-standing then, with the entrance around to one side, and there was only one bay, which was in the center of the facade. The house was expanded in 1832, when the bay on the left side (43 Beacon Street) was built. At about this time the third story was added. The rectangular marble carvings that decorate the building's walls of white Rockport granite are the work of Solomon Willard (1783–1861), the architect of the Bunker Hill Monument in Charlestown. The Somerset Club bought the building in 1871 and moved into it in 1872 after some interior alterations by Snell & Gregerson were completed. An indication of the quality of the club's interior appearance (*opposite*) can be seen in the stairway. The Club was founded in 1852, presumably taking its name from the location of its first clubhouse, at the corner of Beacon and Somerset Streets. The Club today owns, in addition to the granite clubhouse at 42 and 43 Beacon Street, the properties on either side: 41 Beacon Street (built ca. 1838–39) and 44 Beacon Street (built in 1832).

Above: **Little, Brown & Co., 34 Beacon Street. The Parkman House, 33 Beacon Street. The Unitarian Universalist Association, 25 Beacon Street.** Nos. 34 and 33 Beacon Street (the houses on the left end and middle of this block) were built in 1824–25 by Cornelius Coolidge. Mrs. George Parkman bought 33 in 1853. The house stayed in the Parkman family until 1908, when George Francis Parkman bequeathed it to the city. It served for some time as the headquarters of the Boston Park Department, but is now used as a conference center and reception hall for distinguished guests of the city. No. 34 was a private residence for many years, but in 1909 it was acquired by the publishing house of Little, Brown & Co. (established in 1837), which has remained at this location up to the present day. The building on the right, at 25 Beacon Street, was built in 1925–27 for the American Unitarian Association. In 1961 the organization merged with the Universalist Church of America, forming the Unitarian Universalist Association, which has its continental headquarters here.

Opposite, top: **24 Pinckney Street.** The house in the photograph was originally a stable, built in 1802 on the property of Jonathan Mason, one of the Mount Vernon Proprietors. Used as a grocery store in the 1830s, it was converted for use as a residence in 1884. The owner in 1884, Thomas Bailey Aldrich, had William Ralph Emerson (1833–1917) design and remodel the house for him, and it is this architect's work which has earned the

building its name "the house of odd windows." Emerson also designed the Boston Art Club (now the Copley Square High School) on Newbury Street in 1881. No. 24 Pinckney Street has a cross-eyed look about it, with its windows of different sizes set in an asymmetrical design, but there is also a certain exotic appeal in it. The use of this sort of counterpoint in design was in fashion during the 1880s, and the style of architecture with which it is associated is that of the Queen Anne Revival.

Opposite, bottom: **59 Mount Vernon Street.** This house was built in 1837 for Adam Wallace Thaxter. Later in the nineteenth century it was the home of Thomas Bailey Aldrich, who was editor of the *Atlantic Monthly* from 1881 to 1890. It was probably designed by Edward Shaw (b. 1784), one of Boston's most competent architects during the pre–Civil War period, and author of several builder's guides: *Civil Architecture* [1830], *Rural Architecture* [1843], and *The Modern Architect* [1854]. His influence on the architecture of New England through these books was widespread. No. 59 Mount Vernon Street presents the Greek Revival style, in which Shaw worked, in a striking and demonstrative manner. While the portico is comparatively simple and heavy-looking for a house of this period on Beacon Hill, these qualities actually add to its intended effect. Rather than serve as an ornament or as the trimming of an otherwise conservative-looking house, the portico seems to function symbolically, or as an aesthetic gesture of homage to the idealism of classical Greece.

Above: **The Claflin Building, 18–20 Beacon Street.** The Claflin Building was built in 1883–84. Its rugged Richardsonian facade of dark stone, designed by William G. Preston, is one of the more interesting sights on this stretch of Beacon Street. Even more diverting, though, was the occupant of the store at 18, Goodspeed's Book Shop. The famous store was established in 1898, moved to this location in 1936, and finally moved to 7 Beacon Street in 1981. Its original owner and proprietor was Charles Goodspeed, who was the author of an entertaining volume of memoirs entitled *Yankee Bookseller* [1937].

Opposite: **Congregational House, 14 Beacon Street.** The American Congregational Association was organized in 1853 to promote the interests of Congregationalism and to establish a library of the religious history and literature of New England. The Association built the present building on Beacon Street for its own use in 1897–98, and occupied most of its eight stories, the remaining space being leased

to a variety of charitable organizations. The building's brick-and-granite facade, designed by Shepley, Rutan & Coolidge, does not merit much discussion apart from the four relief sculptures that decorate the second story. Each, five feet in height and six in length, is carved in Knoxville marble. All four were designed by the Spanish sculptor Domingo Mora, but only the first was actually executed by him. The Spanish-American War broke out before he could start working on the others, causing him to leave the country out of concern for his friends and family. A Swiss sculptor named Stadler completed the work using Mora's designs. The carving shown here (*bottom*) depicts, as do the other three, one of the principles that governed the lives of the early settlers of New England. It pictures an assembly of 20 men deliberating on the appropriation of funds for a new college (Harvard). Governor Henry Vane points to a clause in the bill; Deputy-Governor John Winthrop sits by his side, watching the proceedings.

Louisburg Square. Louisburg Square is a privately owned plot of green grass and elm trees closed off by a black iron fence and surrounded by a private way that is paved with cobblestones. The red brick houses around the square are joined together in protection of this quiet park. This property, once part of John Singleton Copley's pastureland, was bought in 1796 by the Mount Vernon Proprietors, the real-estate syndicate that developed so much of Beacon Hill. In 1826, Stephen P. Fuller, a surveyor, drew the original plan for the square, though he may have been influenced by a similar plan drawn by Charles Bulfinch 30 years earlier. Bulfinch, in turn, was inspired by the small residential squares of London that he must have seen during his travels. The first house in the square was built in 1834, the last in 1847. Although the houses are not as distinguished in architectural design as those on Beacon Street or Mount Vernon Street, some of them have fine details in the Greek Revival style. Among the people who have lived in these houses are: William Dean Howells, author of *The Rise of Silas Lapham* (No. 4); John Gorham Palfrey, editor of the *North American Review* and author of *The History of New England* (No. 5); Amos Bronson Alcott, educator and writer (No. 10); and Louisa May Alcott, author of *Little Women*, who lived with her father at No. 10. Louisburg Square was named, presumably, after the successful siege of the fortress at Louisburg, Nova Scotia, by Massachusetts militiamen in 1745.

Opposite: **The Boston Athenaeum, 10½ Beacon Street.**
The Boston Athenaeum was organized in 1805 by members of the Anthology Society, a literary club. It was incorporated in 1807, and had its first home on Tremont Street. Between 1807 and 1849, the library was housed in a succession of buildings around the city, but none was ever large or secure enough for the Athenaeum's valuable and expanding collections. In 1847, the cornerstone of the present building was laid. When the construction was completed in 1849, the Athenaeum finally had its permanent home. The new building, designed by Edward Clarke Cabot (1818–1901), is an early example of the Italianate style that was popular in Boston during the middle of the nineteenth century. Its walls of dark brown Paterson sandstone give the facade of the building, for all its textbook perfection of design, a dull and brooding look, as if it were stewing over something, or were indignant at the neighboring office buildings, the shadows of which have turned this end of Beacon Street into a dark and tunnel-like passageway. The interior of the Athenaeum originally consisted of three floors, containing the

library, a sculpture gallery, a museum of natural history and a picture gallery. In 1913 and 1914, when the interior was completely rebuilt and made fireproof, the fourth and fifth floors, designed by Henry Forbes Bigelow, were added. The fifth-floor reading room is pictured *(opposite, bottom)*. The Athenaeum's collections are exceedingly rich, and include, for example, the library of George Washington, purchased in 1848.

Above: **The Tudor Apartments, 34½ Beacon Street.** In his book *A Half Century of Boston Building* [1895], Charles S. Damrell described this building as "one of the handsomest modern family hotels." Designed by S. J. F. Thayer, it was built in 1885–87. The craggy masses of its brick-and-stone facade present an interesting combination of flat and round surfaces. There is almost a sculptural effect in the way that the Joy Street side of the building, particularly, seems to be packed with compressed energy. The name comes from Frederick Tudor, "the ice king," who owned the house that once stood on this site.

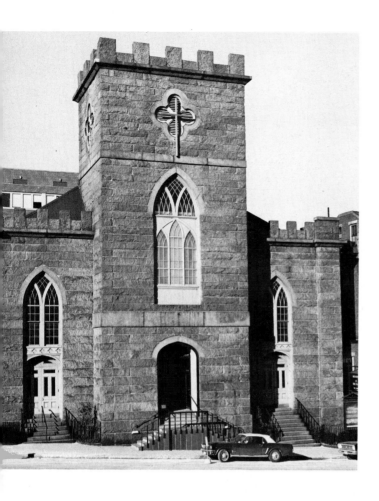

Above, left: **The Church of St. John the Evangelist, 33 Bowdoin Street.** The heavy-set building was built for the Bowdoin Street Congregational Society, a church led by Lyman Beecher that had been organized in 1825. Their meetinghouse, dedicated in 1831, was occupied by the Society until 1862. Its simple Gothic design, with square tower, battlements and rough-hammered granite walls, has been attributed to the architect Solomon Willard. From 1864 to 1883 this building housed the Church of the Advent, an Episcopal church organized in 1844 and inspired by the principles of the Oxford movement in England. Since 1883 the building has been the Mission Church of the Society of St. John the Evangelist.

Above, right: **The Church of the Advent, 30 Brimmer Street.** This building became the new home of the Church of the Advent after it moved from Bowdoin Street. The construction of the church building was begun in 1878. Although it was not completed until 1892, it was ready for use in 1883. Designed by John H. Sturgis (1834–1888) of Sturgis & Brigham, it is a striking example of the High Victorian Gothic style. Its picturesque masses of brick and stone form, with their asymmetrical organization, a perfectly cohesive and unified composition.

Opposite, bottom: **The Old West Church, 131 Cambridge Street.** The Old West Church, at the corner of Lynde and Cambridge Streets, was designed in 1806 by Asher Benjamin (1773–1845). It was built on the site of the wooden meetinghouse that had been of adequate size in 1737 when the West Church was organized, but by 1806 had become too small to hold the growing congregation. The church was consistently liberal and independent throughout its history, and although it was organized as a Congregational Society and remained Congregationalist, it leaned towards Unitarianism; one of its early ministers, Jonathan Mayhew, has even been called "the father of American Unitarianism." By the end of the nineteenth century, the church's membership had dwindled and in 1892 its last service was held. The building was bought by the City of Boston in 1894 and converted for use as a library. From 1896 to 1960 it served as the Cambridge Street branch of the Boston Public Library. In 1964, the building was reopened as a Methodist church, undergoing extensive reconstruction and restoration work in 1964–65. A plan and front elevation view of the building were printed in Benjamin's architectural handbook, *The American Builder's Companion* [Boston, 1806], one of the seven architectural guides that he wrote during his career. Something of Benjamin's style can be learned from his advice on the use of ornamentation, as it appears on page 29 of the book: ". . . as in sculpture, drapery is not estimable, unless its folds are contrived to grace, and indicate the parts and articulations of the body it covers; so in architecture, the most exquisite ornaments lose all their value, if they load, alter, or confuse the form they are designed to enrich and adorn." Benjamin followed his own advice when he designed the West Church. Its form is simple, and its ornamentation serves to accent this form in a decorous and pleasing manner.

Above: **The Charles Street Meeting House, 70 Charles Street.** The Charles Street Meeting House is located at the corner of Charles and Mount Vernon Streets. When it was built for the Third Baptist Church in 1807, its west side nearly abutted the Charles River. It was not until the middle of the nineteenth century that the land west of Charles Street was filled in for several blocks. Designed by Asher Benjamin, the Meeting House is a humble relative of the same architect's Old West Church on Cambridge Street. It is sober and severe in aspect, but the pattern of the large windows in the recessed arches, running from the front of the building around to the sides, has an aesthetic appeal that offsets the severity. In the 1850s the windows on the sides were lengthened and the lower ones shortened to meet the requirements of the new parish rooms that were built below street level, an interior reconstruction that also required the main floor inside the

building to be raised several feet and the pitch of the roof to be made a little steeper. Apart from these alterations, the exterior appearance of the Meeting House today is much as it was in 1807. The building has a place in the history of black people in Boston, as it was here that some of the most well-known antislavery orators (William Lloyd Garrison, Frederick Douglass and Sojourner Truth) spoke. In 1876 the building was sold to the First African Methodist Episcopal Society, a black church that was founded late in the eighteenth century. The Meeting House was threatened in 1920 when Charles Street was widened, but was saved from demolition by a group of Beacon Hill citizens who paid to have the building moved ten feet to the west and away from danger. In 1939 it was bought by the Charles Street Meeting House Society, an organization mindful of historic preservation. Later occupants were the Albanian Orthodox Church of St. John the Evangelist and the Unitarian Universalists. The most recent development in the building's life is the present plan to subdivide the interior for a combination of shops and offices.

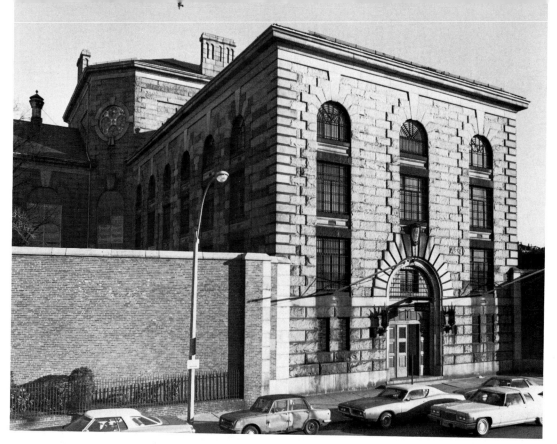

Above: **Charles Street Jail, 215 Charles Street.** Gridley J. F. Bryant designed this dark gray building, with the assistance of the noted prison reformer Rev. Louis Dwight. It was erected in 1850–51 to replace the old jail on Leverett Street, and was considered at the time to be a vast improvement over the older building. The plan of the Charles Street Jail is in the form of a Greek cross, with a central octagonal section and four wings extending out from the center. This plan, along with the placement of 30 arched windows, each 33 feet in height, around all sides of the building, was designed to allow maximum light into each of the 220 cheerless jail cells. The walls of the jail are of Quincy granite. The cells, each eight feet by 11 feet, have floors and ceilings of the same material. The building is still used as a jail, despite recent attempts to shut it down. It retains much of its original appearance, but one notable alteration has been the removal of the lantern that once stood atop the central octagonal section.

Right: **Massachusetts General Hospital, Fruit Street.** Charles Bulfinch designed the main building of the Massachusetts General Hospital (founded in 1799, incorporated in 1811) in 1817. The cornerstone was laid in 1818, and construction of the building, supervised by Alexander Parris, was completed in 1821. Built of Chelmsford granite, the hospital was one of the first granite structures of note in Boston. Bulfinch explained his choice of material in a letter to the hospital's trustees (now in the collection of the Massachusetts Historical Society) written on March 15, 1817: ". . . this material is certainly to be preferred to brick in all situations open to driving storms & sea air. It will be more costly at the beginning, but will be more durable & require fewer repairs; & from the good quality & richness of the materials, will allow of a less decorated stile of ornament." The building's notable features are the Classical portico, with its Ionic columns, inspired by Palladio's Villa Foscati, and the dome (partially obscured) that rises over the old amphitheater. It was in this amphitheater that the first public

demonstration of the use of ether as an anaesthetic was given in 1846. Massachusetts General has changed quite a lot over the years, and consists now of a large complex of buildings that have been erected around the original Bulfinch building. This building itself has undergone several major alterations. In 1844–46, an octagonal addition was built at the rear of the central section. At the same time, the east and west wings were also added, doubling the length of the whole. In 1925–30, the interiors of the two wings were completely reconstructed and made fireproof. Today, the Bulfinch building of the hospital and the State House stand as enduring evidence of one architect's ability to shape a city's institutional life as well as its physical appearance.

South End

The South End was built up between 1850 and 1870 on land that was filled in gradually between 1805 and 1870. The houses in the photograph are 7, 9 and 11 Union Park, built in the 1850s. They have stylistic aspects that recur in many of the townhouses in the South End: the swell-fronts of red brick, the black iron railings and fences, the mansard roofs and the high stoops. By the turn of the century, these townhouses, once very fashionable, had become rooming houses and apartment buildings, housing of poor immigrants. In *The City Wilderness* [1898], edited by Robert A. Woods, the South End is described as it was then: "A very large traffic rumbles through its streets without having any relation to it whatever, and a great part of the stream of people on its sidewalks have neither business duties nor home responsibilities within its borders." *The City Wilderness* is a fascinating book, and gives the reader a Dickensian tour through the South End underworld. There is a chapter titled "Criminal Tendencies," in which one aspect of the area's bad reputation is surveyed: "From whichever side we approach prostitution in our district, we are impressed by its magnitude. It is not too much to say that it has its haunts throughout the length and breadth of the district." Not until the 1960s and 1970s did the South End make its comeback from decline.

Above: **Union Park.** Designed by Ellis S. Chesbrough and William Parrott, Union Park was laid out in 1851. The houses that surround the park were built in the 1850s and are among the finest in the South End. The resemblance to Louisburg Square is strong: the English-style plan, the red brick townhouses and the green park enclosed by a black iron fence; but Union Park is larger than Louisburg Square, and less well known. There is no great social weight in residence here and no signs that say "Private Way." It is exclusive only in that it is expensive to live here, and it is expensive because it is one of the loveliest places in the city.

Opposite, top: **The St. Cloud Hotel, 567 Tremont Street.** Designed originally for "French flats," the St. Cloud Hotel was one of the first apartment buildings in Boston and in the United States. It was built in 1869–70 after plans by Nathaniel J. Bradlee (1829–1888). The marble facade, with its tall windows and projecting pavilions, is in the French Academic style, and possesses some of its original charm, even if it is now somewhat gone in the teeth. The hotel, standing opposite Union Park, was once a very fashionable place to live, but its fortunes declined along with those of the South End. Early in the 1920s it was renamed Comfort Chambers, and functioned as a rooming house, with shops occupying its street level. From around 1926 to the late 1960s the building was called the Park Hotel (also the Park House Hotel). By 1970 it was vacant and in the hands of the Boston Redevelopment Authority. It is still vacant, although dozens of pigeons inhabit the recesses of the facade, and hobos sleep in the doorway. The building is leased to the Boston Center for the Arts, and will soon receive the restoration that it

deserves. In its recycled state it will provide space for residential and commercial use. The B.C.A. also leases and plans renovation for the brick building to the right of the St. Cloud. This is the Mystic River Building, which dates from the 1860s.

Opposite, bottom: **The Boston Center for the Arts, 537–543 Tremont Street.** The main building of the Boston Center for the Arts complex on Tremont Street, originally called the Cyclorama Building, housed the gigantic exhibitions of cyclorama paintings that were very popular in the nineteenth century. The first painting on exhibition here was Paul Philippoteaux's *The Battle of Gettysburg.* It surrounded the viewer on all sides, forming a circle around him 400 feet in diameter, and looming over him 50 feet. Built in 1884, the building was designed by Cumming & Sears, the same firm that designed the New Old South Church in Copley Square and the Bedford building downtown. Mary Van Meter, in a report written for the Massachusetts Historical Commission, described the original facade as being "built in a Victorian feudal style with keep and guard tower." Behind the facade is the enormous rotunda, and over the rotunda is a great dome with a glass oculus. In 1899 the building was leased to the New England Vehicle Transportation Company, for use as a garage. It was here that Albert Champion invented the Champion sparkplug. In 1922 the building was sold to the Commercial Flower Exchange, and was used as a flower market for several decades. It was leased by the Boston Redevelopment Authority in 1970 to the Boston Center for the Arts, was renovated in the early 1970s by Eco-Tecture International, and now provides space for exhibitions, flea markets and events of all kinds.

Opposite, top: **The Piano Craft Guild, 791 Tremont Street.** Formerly the piano factory of Jonas Chickering & Sons, The Piano Craft Guild was built in 1853–54 to replace the old Chickering factory on Washington Street, which burnt in 1852. Jonas Chickering was a self-made man who started in business in 1823 and went on to build his enterprise into an internationally known institution. The new factory that he built was one of many piano factories in the South End, but it was the largest of them by far, employing over 400 people. It was said to be the largest factory under one roof on the continent, and the largest building of any kind in the country, excepting the U.S. Capitol. Designed by Edwin Payson, it was constructed of brick and stone, with its five-story walls forming an enormous horseshoe. A contemporary observer of the building as it was being constructed wrote: "The raw materials will enter at one door, and passing successively through every department, will pass out of another door at the other extremity of the building, in a state of perfect completion." Chickering never lived to see the building finished. After his death in 1853, his sons took over the business and ran it successfully for many decades. In the 1930s, the building was sold, and the Chickering business moved to New York. After that, the building was shared by about a dozen different companies at any given time. In 1973 and 1974 it was renovated and converted to space for 174 studios and apartments by the firm of Gelardin, Bruner, Cott, Inc., with help from Anderson Notter Associates. It now enjoys a new life as the Piano Craft Guild.

Opposite, bottom: **The Youth's Companion Building, 209 Columbus Avenue. The Cahners Building, 221 Columbus Avenue.** The *Youth's Companion* was a weekly children's magazine that was founded in 1827 by Nathaniel Willis and Asa Rand. It remained in publication for 102 years, and was enormously popular, having a circulation figure near 500,000 in the 1890s. It appealed to adults as well as children, with stories and poems by such writers as Rudyard Kipling, Walt Whitman, Jack London and Jules Verne. The large building on the right in the photograph was built for the *Youth's Companion* in 1890–92. It was designed by the firm of H. W. Hartwell

& W. C. Richardson. Its Romanesque elements exhibit the influence of H. H. Richardson in the massive piers and arches on the upper stories and the broad Syrian arches below. The material used for the facade was a buff-colored brick for the upper stories, and red Longmeadow sandstone for the first story. This building's neighbor to the left is the Cahners Building. Originally it was the Pope Manufacturing Company Building, where "Columbia" bicycles were made. Albert A. Pope founded this company in 1879; it was he who is credited with popularizing the bicycle in America. In the 1890s, the Pope Company was the largest manufacturer of bicycles in the world. The Pope Building was built in 1891, then rebuilt in 1896, after a fire burnt it down. It was designed in both its original and reconstructed state by the firm of Peabody & Stearns. The facade, in Italian Renaissance Revival style, is of limestone and brick, with terra-cotta ornamentation. The building has been the home of the Cahners Publishing Company since the early 1960s.

Above: **Franklin Square House, 11 East Newton Street.** Franklin Square House was originally the St. James Hotel, built in 1867–68 by M. M. Ballou of *Ballou's Pictorial*, with John R. Hall as architect. With 400 rooms, it was the largest hotel in the city and one of the most elegant. The grand facade was designed in the French Second Empire style, exhibiting a precise symmetry of decorative columns and pilasters, projecting pavilions and crowning mansard roof. In 1882 the building was sold to the New England Conservatory of Music, which used it as a dormitory for women, as well as for classroom and office space. In 1902 the Conservatory moved to another location, and the building became a residence for self-supporting working women. Renamed Franklin Square House, it continued in its function as a women's residence for many decades. The building was owned by the city between 1970 and 1975, when it was used by the city government for a variety of community offices. Then, in 1975 and 1976, it was renovated by its new owner, the State Street Development Company, and converted by the Boston Architectural Team and Archplan, Inc., to a complex of 193 apartments for elderly citizens.

The Boston Fire Department Headquarters, 60 Bristol Street. The Charles C. Perkins School, 139 St. Botolph Street. Edmund March Wheelwright, City Architect of Boston in the 1890s, was responsible for many of the schoolhouses, fire stations and police stations that survive from the period. His schoolhouses were particularly distinguished for their practicality of design and their discreet aesthetic appeal. One example is the Charles C. Perkins School *(above)* on the corner of St. Botolph and Cumberland Streets in the South End. It was built in 1891–92, and was converted recently for condominium use by Graham Gund. Another example of Wheelwright's work for the City is the former Fire Department Headquarters, built in 1894 *(left)*. It was used for many years as a firemen's training school where trainees were taught in their rescue drills to scuttle up the sides of the building's tower, modeled on that of the Palazzo Vecchio in Florence. Since 1980 the building has been occupied by an organization called the Pine Street Inn, which runs a shelter for homeless men and women.

Above: **The Dover Street Station, Dover Street at Washington Street.** Boston's subway system was the first of its kind in the country. Originally it was privately owned and operated, although the tunnels for the subway were built by the Boston Transit Commission (an ancestor of the present Massachusetts Bay Transportation Authority). The first section of the system, running from Park Street Station to the Public Garden, was completed in 1897. Between 1899 and 1901, the elevated line between Sullivan Square in Charlestown and Dudley Street in Roxbury was built, and one station on that line, the Dover Street Station, is shown here. Designed by an unidentified architect, this station's exterior, made of copper paneling, is decorated in a pleasing manner that is surprising for such a utilitarian structure. As one of the small number of early subway stations that have survived to the present day, the Dover Street Station has been recognized as a historic structure, and, it is hoped, will be preserved as such.

Right: **The First Corps of Cadets Armory, Columbus Avenue at Arlington Street.** The First Corps of Cadets was chartered in 1741 to serve as a bodyguard to the governor. The Cadets have since been used in the suppression of civil disturbances of various kinds, including those during the union movements of the late nineteenth century and the police strike of 1919. Their granite fortress in the South End was designed by William G. Preston, and was built in 1891–97. Its medieval aspects—the battlements, the turrets, the drawbridge—are an example of nineteenth-century predilection for the deliberately archaic. The building was sold in 1965 to Fitz-Inn Auto Parks, Inc., and from 1966 to 1973 it was leased to the University of Massachusetts for use as a library. In

1980 it was sold to the owners of the Boston Park Plaza Hotel, who renamed it The Plaza Castle, and converted it for use as an office building and exhibition hall.

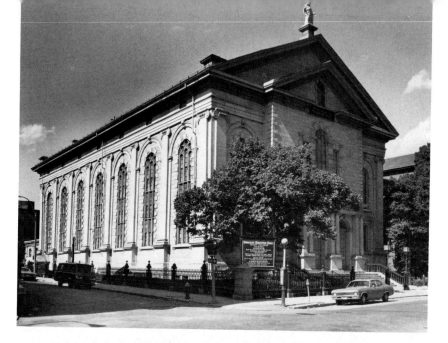

Top: **The Church of the Immaculate Conception, 761 Harrison Avenue.** The Church of the Immaculate Conception, located on the corner of Harrison Avenue and Concord Street, is one of the finest buildings in the South End. It was built by the Jesuits in 1858–61, and was designed by Patrick C. Keeley (1816–1896), also the architect of the Holy Cross Cathedral on Washington Street. Its walls of white New Hampshire granite exhibit features of the Italianate style. The classic elegance of the interior is the work of Arthur Gilman. Of particular note is the concert organ, which dates from 1863, and is considered to be one of the best in the country.

Bottom: **Theodore Parker Memorial Hall, 49 Berkeley Street.** This Victorian monster, located at the corner of Berkeley and Appleton Streets, was the meeting place of the Twenty-eighth Congregational Society of Boston, a Unitarian church founded by Theodore Parker in 1845. Designed by an unidentified architect, it was built in 1872–73. Although never very important historically, the building has served in an unusually wide variety of capacities throughout its life. It was known as the Theodore Parker Memorial Hall from 1872 until 1922, functioning at various times as a church, a lecture hall, a cooking and sewing school and a Jewish community center. During the 1920s and 1930s it was called the Caledonian building, and provided space for the Caledonian Club, the British Naval & Military Veterans Association (ca. 1930), the Sieveling Dana School of the Dance (ca. 1930) and other organizations. Later, it housed the Church of Jesus and the Volunteers of America. In the 1960s and early 1970s it was named the Magna Building. Its occupants during this period were Magna Film Productions, Inc., the Telavix Recording Studios and the Boston Tea Party, a psychedelic rock nightclub (late 1960s). A fire in 1973 burnt much of its interior, but in 1974–75 it was rebuilt by the Boston Architectural Team. Now called the Berkeley Center, it contains a laundromat in the basement, a food store on the first floor and 33 apartments on the upper floors.

The Fenway District

The Fenway is a tree-lined street that wends its way around a park called the Fens. This park was once a very foul, marshy area, but was transformed in the 1880s to its present arboreous state by the noted landscape architect Frederick Law Olmsted (1822–1903). Through the center of the Fens flows the Muddy River, shown here. Arched over the river is the Boylston Street Bridge, built ca. 1881–84, and attributed to H. H. Richardson. Most of the buildings that surround the Fens are apartment houses, but there are also, on the Fenway and on the connecting streets, some of the country's most distinguished institutions—great libraries, museums, schools, churches and hospitals. Most of these institutions were built around the turn of the century, during what seemed to be a very promising period for the Fenway. Later, for a number of reasons, not the least of which was the building of the Massachusetts Turnpike through the park, the district declined. The next few years could see important improvements, however, if the efforts of various neighborhood activists are able to make the community more conscious of itself.

Opposite, top: **Symphony Hall, 301 Massachusetts Avenue.** The widely celebrated Boston Symphony Orchestra, founded in 1881 by Henry Lee Higginson, had as its first concert hall the Music Hall (now the Orpheum Theatre), on Hamilton Place. In the 1890s, because this building was, for various reasons, inadequate to the needs of the B.S.O., funds were raised for the construction of a new hall. The new Symphony Hall, at the corner of Massachusetts and Huntington Avenues, opened in 1900, a masterpiece of acoustical design, very happily received by the public. Less enthusiastically received was the building's exterior, a top-heavy composition of Greek Revival and Italian Renaissance elements that seems awkward and soulless. The architect, Charles F. McKim, of McKim, Mead and White, was also architect of the Boston Public Library. McKim's original plan for the hall was scrapped. Even with the design that was accepted, though, there were compromises.

Opposite, bottom: **The Museum of Fine Arts, 465 Huntington Avenue.** The Museum of Fine Arts is one of the great art museums of the world. It was founded in 1870, and had its first building in Copley Square. By the turn of the century, the museum's collections had expanded so much that it became necessary to construct a larger home for them. In 1906, the architectural plans for the new building, the work of Guy Lowell who was assisted by R. Clipston Sturgis, Edmund M. Wheelright and D. Despradelle, were approved. Designed in a neo-Classical style, the building exhibits the conservatism and restraint in expression that are typical of the architecture of this period. The facade is long and low, but the columns of the portico, as well as the tall windows that run along the front and sides, offset this horizontal sprawling aspect.

The building was completed in 1909, with about half of the space on the site left vacant for future expansion. Much of this space is now occupied by the Evans Memorial Wing, built in 1911–15, and the Decorative Arts Wing, built in 1924–28. These two extensions overlook the Fenway and, like the facade on Huntington Avenue, have walls made of Crotch Island granite. A new west wing, designed by I. M. Pei, was completed in 1981.

Above: **The Gardner Museum, 280 The Fenway.** Isabella Stewart Gardner and her husband, John Lowell Gardner, were avid collectors of art. Their immense wealth enabled them to collect with limitless extravagance. During the 1890s they talked of building a museum for their collection, but plans never progressed beyond the hiring of an architect, Willard T. Sears (1837–1920), to make preliminary drawings for the building. When Mr. Gardner died in 1898, it was left to Mrs. Gardner to supervise the project through to its completion. She bought land on the Fenway, at Worthington Road, and had Sears design for her a Venetian palace, built to her specifications, accommodating her personal tastes and eccentricities. The building, named Fenway Court, consisted of four stories (the top floor for living quarters, the lower floors for the museum) around a large glass-enclosed courtyard. Mrs. Gardner oversaw the application of the most subtle of ornaments, and had the builders fit into the building various architectural fragments that the Gardners had found in Europe during their travels. Every corner of the building reveals another aspect of this woman's strong personality. The museum was incorporated in 1900, and its construction was completed in 1902. Its opening on January 1, 1903, was one of the great events in Boston's social history.

The Christian Science Center, Massachusetts Avenue.
The Christian Science Center is a vast complex of buildings, located off Massachusetts Avenue in the Fenway district, serving as the home of the First Church of Christ, Scientist. The Church was founded in 1879 by Mary Baker Eddy. Its first church building, constructed in 1893–94, and designed by Franklin I. Welch, is called the Mother Church. It is tucked behind the Mother Church Extension, which dwarfs the original church. The Extension Building *(opposite, top)*, a great domed structure faced with limestone from Bedford, Indiana, dates from 1906. At its dedication, Mary Baker Eddy was moved to say in her message for the occasion: "Methinks this church is the one edifice on earth which most prefigures self-abnegation, hope, faith; love catching a glimpse of glory." The building was designed by Charles E. Brigham (d. 1925) and Solon S. Beman (1853–1914), and presents a

jumble of architectural features that are of Byzantine and Italian Renaissance origin. The huge semicircular portico was added in 1975, according to a Church brochure, "to provide a larger, more convenient entrance." The Christian Science Publishing Society Building *(opposite, bottom)* is the home of the *Christian Science Monitor*, a well-respected newspaper that was founded by Mrs. Eddy in 1908. The building was designed by Chester Churchill, and was built in 1932–35. The most recent additions to the Christian Science Center are the new Sunday School building (completed in 1971), the Church Colonnade (completed in 1973; *above*), which houses the Church's communications departments, and the new Church Administration Building (completed in1973). These three concrete buildings, all of them the work of the architects I. M. Pei and Araldo Cossutta, surround a long reflecting pool to form an unlovely, graceless group.

Above: **Boston State College, 625 Huntington Avenue.**
The history of Boston State College begins in 1851, when
the Boston City Council passed an act establishing the
Boston Normal School for young women. The school later
admitted men, and was known by the successive names of
the Teachers' College of the City of Boston, the State
Teachers' College of Boston and, since 1968, Boston State
College. The latest addition to the B.S.C. campus on
Huntington Avenue is the Tower Building, designed by
C. E. Maguire and constructed in 1976. The attractive
building is used for the college library, classrooms and a
cafeteria. Its form looks charmingly asymmetrical, as if it
had been assembled by an ambitious child, but its sleek
black surface of tinted glass also gives it an air of cool
sophistication.

Opposite, top: **Horticultural Hall, 300 Massachusetts
Avenue.** The Massachusetts Horticultural Society is the
second oldest horticultural society in America, having
been founded in 1829. The Horticultural Hall on Massachusetts Avenue at Huntington Avenue was built by the
society in 1900–1901, and was designed by the firm of
Wheelwright & Haven. Douglass Tucci, in his book *Built
in Boston* [1978], offered the opinion that the hall "may be
the handsomest English Baroque building in the city.
. . ." It functions as an exhibition hall and lecture hall,
and aids the Society in its efforts to widen public apprecia-
tion of the natural environment.

Opposite, bottom: **Massachusetts Historical Society, 1154
Boylston Street.** The Massachusetts Historical Society,
founded in 1791, is the oldest historical society in the
United States. It houses one of the country's finest collections of books and manuscripts, among which are the
papers of Presidents John Adams and John Quincy
Adams, the papers of the Winthrop and Revere families,
and the architectural drawings of Thomas Jefferson. After
it moved to its present home, the society shared some of
its rooms with the American Academy of Arts and
Sciences for several years, until the academy built its own
headquarters on Newbury Street. The society's building,
at the corner of Boylston Street and the Fenway, was
designed by Edmund March Wheelwright (1854–1912),
and was completed in 1899. Wheelwright, of the Boston
firm of Wheelwright & Haven, was also the architect of
Horticultural Hall and many other buildings around the
city. The society's building offers the neighborhood a corner of quiet and intellectual calm, with its graceful and
dignified proportions, and it could be considered Wheelwright's best work. The facade, of "spotted" light brown
brick and hand-cut limestone, was designed in the
Renaissance Revival style that was fashionable at the turn
of the century. Some enlargement of the building was
undertaken in 1948, and in 1972 a large addition of the
rear was completed.

Back Bay

Most of the buildings of the Back Bay district were erected during the second half of the nineteenth century on a landfill that had begun in 1857 and continued for several decades. The landfill was, for its time, one of the most awesome and ambitious urban projects ever undertaken. In aesthetic terms, its conception was visionary and idealistic. The streets were laid out in emulation of the great avenues of Paris, with the same grandness of scale and symmetry of design. The street plan, designed by Arthur Gilman (1821–1882), called for five long avenues running parallel to the Charles River, with cross streets intersecting at regular intervals. The middle avenue of the five, Commonwealth Avenue, is one of the finest streets in America. It is 240 feet wide, and has a tree-lined park running down its center, ornamented in several places with statues, such as the one seen here of William Lloyd Garrison *(above)*, by Olin Levi Warner (1886). Lining this avenue and the other four are the buildings of Back Bay: the townhouses, churches, schools and other institutions that have made this district famous. Taken in their collective entirety, these buildings are a tribute to civilization and to the art of architecture. And, as Bainbridge Bunting wrote in *Houses of Boston's Back Bay* [1967]: ". . . the Back Bay has a thousand associations with American thought and action of the later nineteenth century. In brownstone and brick it symbolizes its epoch in a way that words and figures alone cannot."

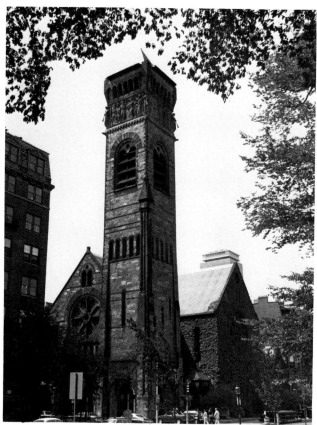

Above, left: **The First Baptist Church, 110 Commonwealth Avenue.** The First Baptist Church, standing on the corner of Clarendon Street and Commonwealth Avenue, was built in 1870–73. The Church was originally Unitarian, home of the Brattle Square Society, but it was bought by the First Baptist Society in 1882, following the dissolution of the Unitarian congregation. The building is an early great work of the noted architect Henry Hobson Richardson (1838–1886). Its walls are of Roxbury puddingstone; its forms an adaption of Romanesque styles. The tower is unforgettable: "a fairy tale," as Louis Sullivan once wrote. Mariana Griswold Van Rensselaer, author of *Henry Hobson Richardson and His Works* [1888], admired its "magnificent independence—the way it rises in a single spring from its own sturdy feet." Above the arches of its belfry is a frieze which represents in its four sections Baptism, Communion, Marriage and Death. The frieze was designed by Frédéric Auguste Bartholdi (the sculptor who is most famous for the Statue of Liberty), after a sketch by Richardson.

Above, right: **The Ritz-Carlton Hotel, 15 Arlington Street.** The Ritz-Carlton Hotel is located at the corner of Arlington and Newbury Streets, overlooking the Public Garden. It was built in 1926–27, after designs by the firm of Strickland, Blodget & Law. Its exterior is not much to look at, but because of its excellent location and high-class service, it is one of the most fashionable hotels in the city. An enormous 17-story addition to the Ritz, designed by Skidmore, Owings & Merrill, was completed in 1981.

Opposite: **Arlington Street Church, 355 Boylston Street.** The religious society called the Arlington Street Church was originally the First Presbyterian Church, also known as "the Church of Presbyterian Strangers," and was founded in 1729 by a small group of immigrants from Ireland and Scotland. Its first meeting house was on Long Lane, now Federal Street. When the street's name changed late in the eighteenth century, the church adopted the name Federal Street Church; when the present building on the corner of Arlington and Boylston Streets was dedicated in 1861, it became the Arlington Street Church. In 1786 the Church adopted the tenets of Congregationalism; under the leadership of William Ellery Channing from 1803 to 1842, it became Unitarian. At the present time, the Church is affiliated with the Unitarian-Universalists. The building was designed by Arthur Gilman, assisted by Gridley J. F. Bryant, in the Georgian style of Christopher Wren, with influence and inspiration coming from the architecture of the Italian Renaissance. It is built of a dark freestone from Newark, New Jersey. In the *Boston Evening Transcript* of December 6, 1861, Gilman described the new church and set forth some of his architectural principles at the same time: ". . . the essential ideas of [a composition] should be symmetry, regularity, and a harmonious and even balance of the leading lines and masses of structure." More specifically ". . . the tower and spire of the church . . . are placed symmetrically in the center of the principal front of the building. This is a wide departure from the practice of tucking them to one corner, so prevalent of late years . . . ." Gilman's rationalistic no-nonsense approach to his art produced in the Arlington Street Church a work of somber aspect and understated elegance.

Opposite: **The John Hancock Tower, corner of St. James Avenue and Clarendon Street.** The John Hancock Tower, the home office of the John Hancock Mutual Life Insurance Company, stands high over Copley Square in Back Bay. Designed by I. M. Pei & Partners, with Henry N. Cobb as Partner-in-Charge, it was built by the Gilbane Building Company of Providence, Rhode Island. The groundbreaking for the tower was in 1968; construction was completed in 1976. It is the tallest building in New England, rising 790 feet in 60 stories. Each of its four enormous walls, which form a rhomboid, is a wide glass curtain that reflects with perfect clarity the city and sky around it. The tower's north side is a mirror reflection of Trinity Church, and on its west side is the Copley Plaza Hotel (seen here). The gray-tinted tempered safety glass is framed in black aluminum. On a cold and cloudy day, the glass appears grayish-green and impenetrable, but on a sunny warm day, the icy surface turns a liquid blue and mirrors the sky so well that the tower at times becomes almost invisible. During a sunset,

the tower can reflect in a striking way long streaks of orange and red. It is the culmination of a long architectural movement toward simplicity and honesty in design. Free from the concept of facade and nineteenth-century ornamentation, it is a product of a more modern idealism, a representative of the American space age. Suzannah Lessard has written of the John Hancock Tower and other "towers of light," and has remarked that they are "already a period piece of our immediate past," coming out of "a moment in our history when power and optimism converged."

Above: **The old John Hancock Building, 200 Berkeley Street (corner of Stuart Street).** The old John Hancock Building was erected in 1945–49, and was designed in the Art Deco style by the firm of Cram & Ferguson. For two decades, the tubby 26-story structure was the tallest building in the city, and was a sort of Bostonian equivalent to New York City's Empire State Building.

Trinity Church, Copley Square. Trinity Church, founded in 1773, was the third Episcopal church in Boston, after King's Chapel and Christ Church. Trinity's first church building was downtown on Summer Street; its second was on the same site. Its third and present home is the magnificent building in Copley Square *(above)*, designed by H. H. Richardson. It is Richardson's masterpiece and one of America's greatest works of architecture. Construction was begun in 1873; its cornerstone was laid in 1875, and in 1877 the church was consecrated. The portico and front towers on the western side were added in 1896–97 (Shepley, Rutan & Coolidge, architects). A light Dedham granite and red Longmeadow sandstone were the building materials. Interior decorations are by John La Farge, among others. In his *Description of the Church*

[1877], Richardson wrote: "The style of the Church may be characterized as a free rendering of the French Romanesque, inclining particularly to the school that flourished in the eleventh century in Central France—the ancient Aquitaine—which, secure, politically, on the one hand from the Norman pirates, and on the other from the Moorish invasions, as well as architecturally emancipated from the influence of the classical traditions and examples which still ruled the southern provinces, developed in various forms a system of architecture of its own, differing from the classical manner in that, while it studied elegance, it was also constructional, and from the succeeding Gothic, in that, although constructional, it could sacrifice something of mechanical dexterity for the sake of grandeur and repose."

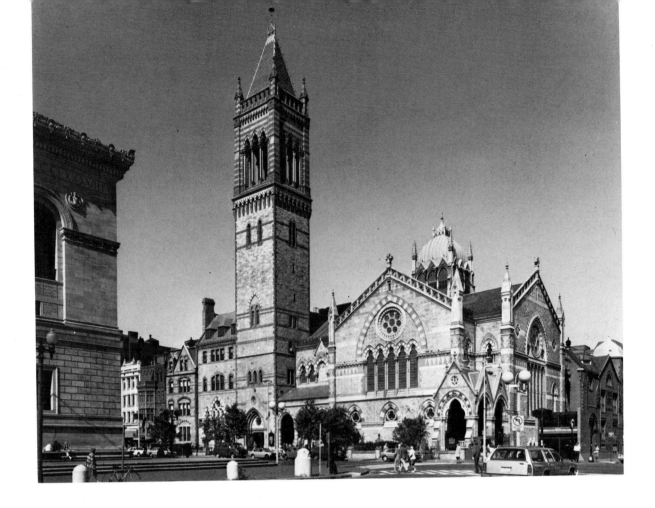

Opposite: **The Boston Public Library, Copley Square.**
The Boston Public Library on Dartmouth Street, facing
Copley Square, was created for an expanding collection of
books that would no longer fit the old library building on
Boylston Street. The City of Boston acquired the land for
the new library from the Commonwealth in 1880. Construction began in 1888 and was completed in 1894. The
library was designed by Charles Follen McKim (1847–
1909) of the New York architectural firm McKim, Mead
and White, and was built by Woodbury & Leighton, of
Boston. McKim drew inspiration for his design from the
great palaces of the Italian Renaissance and from Henri
Labrouste's Bibliothèque Ste. Geneviève in Paris, among
other works. There was also some intention to offset the
Romanesque design of H. H. Richardson's Trinity
Church, on the opposite side of the square, with the
serenity of Classical proportions. The library's great
arched windows, inspired by the arches of the Colosseum
in Rome, are set into a long rectangular facade of smooth
white granite. The roof, of dark red tile, is topped with a
copper cresting. At the front entrance of the library are
the two bronze figures, *Art* and *Science*, by the sculptor
Bela L. Pratt. Among the other artists who contributed to
the decoration of the building's exterior and interior are
John Singer Sargent, Daniel Chester French, Augustus
Saint-Gaudens, Pierre Puvis de Chavannes and Edwin
Austin Abbey. The Boston Public Library was a collaborative effort, built in the spirit of the Renaissance. It has
been called "a palace for the people," having been built,
supported and paid for by the people of Boston.

Above: **The New Old South Church, 645 Boylston
Street.** The New Old South Church building, located at
the corner of Boylston and Dartmouth Streets, was built
in 1874–75 as a replacement for the Old South Meeting
House on Washington Street. It was designed by the firm
of Cummings & Sears in a very flamboyant style that was
popular around this time, the North Italian Gothic. The
architects were inspired, in their use of this style, by the
writings of John Ruskin, whose *The Seven Lamps of Architecture* [1849] and *The Stones of Venice* [1851–53] had wide influence over the Romantic movements of the late nineteenth century. One of Ruskin's ideas was that "the most
beautiful things in the world are the most useless . . . ,"
which translates, in architectural terms, into an interest in
the surfaces of buildings as opposed to their structural integrity or function. The New Old South Church is very
Ruskinian. Its surfaces are beautified by ornament, its
details carved by master craftsmen and its walls have the
kind of polychromatic stonework that Ruskin admired so
much in the North Italian Gothic. The walls of the church
building are of Roxbury pudding stone, with trimmings
of brown Connecticut and light Ohio freestone, and there
is an admirable precision and artistic effort implicit in
their design. The great tower, although not the original, is
another prominent feature of New Old South. The first,
similar to the present one in style, but much heavier and
about 15 feet higher, was built on an inadequate foundation, and was found, several years after it was completed,
to be leaning toward the southwest at the rate of about one
inch per year. By 1931, when it was taken down, it was
leaning by about three feet, and was considered danger-
ous. The present tower, completed in 1938, retains much
of its predecessor's original stone.

Opposite: **The Copley Plaza Hotel, Copley Square.** On the south side of Copley Square (the site of the old Museum of Fine Arts) is the Copley Plaza Hotel, one of the finest hotels in the city. Designed by Henry J. Hardenbergh and Clarence H. Blackall, it was opened to the public in 1912. The blankness of expression of the brick and limestone Edwardian-style facade seems to work to the hotel's advantage, giving the impression that behind the conservative gray walls is a limitless reserve of good taste.

Above: **Huntington Avenue at Blagden Street.** This block of buildings, located off Copley Square, has a peculiar appeal when seen from this angle. The tall building at the rear is the Prudential Center tower (built 1960–70; Charles Luckman & Associates, architects), which was, for several years before the completion of the John Hancock Tower, the tallest building in the city. It is useful as an office building and serviceable as a landmark, but because of the unimaginative design of its form, the Prudential is no one's favorite work of architecture.

Opposite, top: **Bonwit Teller, 235 Berkeley Street.** The Boston Society of Natural History, founded in 1830, erected this building in 1862–64 to house its Museum of Natural History, as well as to provide space for its library and lecture hall. It was designed by William G. Preston (1844–1910) who was assisted by his father, Jonathan Preston (1801–88). In the Society's *Proceedings* for 1864 the building is described: "It is built in the classic style of architecture, with Corinthian pilasters and capitals. The foundation of the building is of heavy hammered granite; the first story of freestone, and the second and third of brick, with walls three feet in thickness, having an air space in the interior . . . . On the keys of the front windows of the first story are cut heads of the lion, the bear, the boar and the zebra . . . ." These heads were later removed, unfortunately. The building has been occupied by the Bonwit Teller store since 1947.

Opposite, bottom: **The Berkeley Building, 420 Boylston Street.** One might think that Codman & Despradelle, the architects of this building on the corner of Berkeley and Boylston Streets, had gone too far in their use of ornamented white terra-cotta "icing," if it weren't for the wide bay windows between the icing, which have an airy and very pleasant countereffect. The building, dating from 1906, functions as a center for the decorative arts.

Above: **The Exeter Street Theatre, 26 Exeter Street.** The Exeter Street Theatre, originally the First Spiritual Temple, was built in 1884–85 for the Church of the Working Union of Progressive Spiritualists. The church had its origins in the spiritualist movement of the 1840s, and was based on Christian beliefs, in part, but its members believed also in "the higher intelligences" —spirits that could materialize and speak with the aid of human mediums. An account of the First Spiritual Temple's dedication ceremony in 1885 informs the reader that an Astral Spirit materialized for the occasion, appearing out of nowhere in the darkened auditorium "like a column of phosphorescent light." The temple was designed by the firm of Hartwell & Richardson, and presents a heavy, garrison-like version of the Romanesque style. Its two-toned walls, made of Braggville granite and Longmeadow freestone, resemble the walls of H. H. Richardson's Trinity Church, with their rough-hammered surfaces and similar color-combination. In 1913 Clarence H. Blackall converted the temple's interior for use as a movie theater which has been in continuous operation to the present. A more recent alteration was made in 1974–75, when a glass-enclosed restaurant was added to the building on its Newbury Street side. The firm of Childs, Bertman & Tseckares Associates designed this addition.

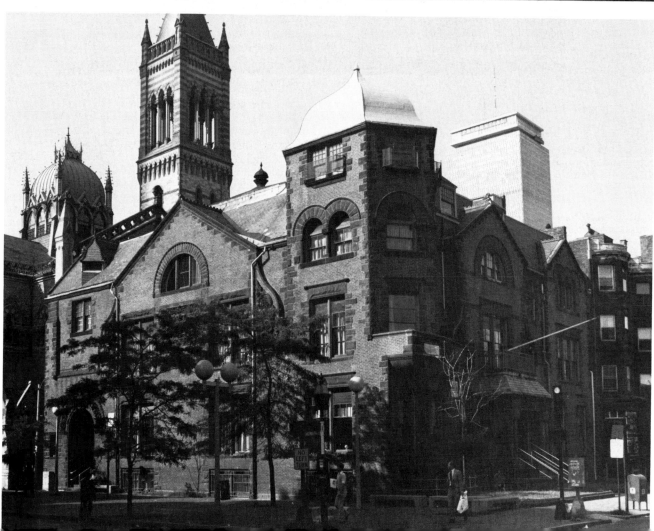

Opposite, top: **The Hotel Agassiz, 191 Commonwealth Avenue.** Henry Lee Higginson, the founder and principal benefactor of the Boston Symphony Orchestra, is remembered also for his gifts to Harvard University and the Museum of Fine Arts. In 1872 he built the large building on the corner of Commonwealth Avenue and Exeter Street, which was one of the first apartment-hotels to appear in Boston. He named it after his wife, Ida Agassiz, whose father was the famous zoologist Louis Agassiz. The building, designed by the firm of Weston & Rand, is made of brick and brownstone, with Gothic features. It functions still as an apartment building.

Opposite, bottom: **The Boston Art Club, 270 Dartmouth Street.** The Boston Art Club was organized in 1854 for the purpose of promoting art through exhibitions and other activities. Its clubhouse on the corner of Dartmouth and Newbury Streets, built in 1881–82, was designed in the Queen Anne Revival style by William Ralph Emerson, with Edward Clarke Cabot as consultant. The building's walls are of dark red brick and sandstone, with elaborate decorations in terra-cotta. The asymmetrical massing and the eccentric fenestration make for an admirably original composition, but one can't help feeling queasy over such an unmeasured ingestion of the exotic. The building is now the Copley Square High School, having been converted for the school's use in 1970 by the Coletti Brothers.

Above: **The Hotel Victoria, 275 Dartmouth Street.** Across the street from the school stands the former Hotel Victoria, another red-brick and terra-cotta creation. Designed by John Lyman Faxon and opened in 1886, it functions now as a combination of shops on street level and condominiums on the upper floors.

Above: **The Hotel Vendome, 160 Commonwealth Avenue.** The former Hotel Vendome, at the corner of Dartmouth Street and Commonwealth Avenue, was named after the palace in France built by Henri IV for his son, the Duc de Vendôme. The hotel was designed by William G. Preston, and its white marble facade is an elegant example of the French Second Empire style. The hotel's first owner and manager, Col. J. W. Wolcott, opened its doors to the public in 1872. The large section of the building (on the right in the photograph), added in 1881, was designed by J. F. Ober. Wolcott entertained the wealthiest and most celebrated persons of the period, charging them $5 a day. Among his guests over the years were Presidents Grant, Harrison, Cleveland and McKinley, as well as the greatest artists, actors and writers. King's *Handbook of Boston* for 1883 is effusive in praise of the hotel: "The plumbing-work is almost marvellous; for every improvement to secure health and comfort has been introduced. Every apartment has access to a spacious bath-room, which, as well as every gas-fixture, has its independent ventilating-tubes. Every room is provided with open fire-places, although the whole building is heated by steam. The registers serve a double purpose—supplying either ventilation or warmth, the change being made by simply turning the knob to the right or to the left. In short, there is hardly an improvement of modern times that has not been introduced into this noble edifice." Electric lights were installed by Thomas Edison in 1882, the first for a public building in Boston. In 1975 the hotel suffered a fire that burnt much of its southeastern section just as it was undergoing extensive renovation and conversion to condominium apartments. The burnt section (on the far left in this 1979 photograph) was replaced by a modern addition by Stahl-Bennett, and the interior renovation was carried out by Irving Salsberg Associates.

Opposite, top: **The Somerset Apartments, 400 Commonwealth Avenue.** The former Somerset Hotel was built in 1897, and was designed by the architect Arthur Bowditch. With its red tile roof, its smooth walls of limestone, and its elegantly styled entrance and windows, this building was one of the handsomest and most desirable hotels in the city. (The Beatles stayed here in 1966!) The firm of Childs, Bertman & Tseckares Associates converted it to an apartment house in 1973–74.

Opposite, bottom: **Charlesgate Hall, 4 Charlesgate East.** Many fashionable apartment-hotels sprang up in the Back Bay district at the end of the nineteenth century. The Hotel Charlesgate, built in 1891 at the corner of Beacon Street and Charlesgate East, was designed by the architect John Pickering Putnam (1847–1917). Its walls are of brick and sandstone, and are ornamented with carved stone facings. A newspaper article of 1891, written while the building was still under construction, describes some of the living arrangements in this kind of apartment house: "The rooms will be exceptionally large, and the greater suites will have kitchens, and will be otherwise arranged for housekeeping, with the alternative of using the general dining rooms, or of having meals served by the house, catered in the private dining rooms attached to the suites." From 1947 to 1972 the building was a student residence owned by Boston University. Since then it has been an apartment house.

Above, left: **The Algonquin Club, 217 Commonwealth Avenue.** The Algonquin Club, on Commonwealth Avenue between Exeter and Fairfield Streets, is one of the great social and dining clubs that sprang up in Boston during the 1870s and 1880s. Its clubhouse was designed by Stanford White (1853–1906) of McKim, Mead and White, and its construction was completed in 1888, with some minor alterations made in 1889. The facade, of granite and Indiana limestone, is an early example of the Italian Renaissance Revival style in Boston, with its Palladian windows, decorative stone carvings and careful symmetry in design. The Club itself was organized in 1885, and was named after the Algonquin Indian nation, the great family of tribes that included those of New England. The club, famous for its sumptuous interiors and its fine food, has attracted an exclusive membership of bankers, lawyers, railroad magnates and merchants. During World War II, when the U.S. and British governments needed an impenetrable fortress of privacy and secrecy in which their early experiments with radar could be conducted, they settled on Boston's Algonquin Club as the logical choice. The scientists used a secret stairway to get to their quarters, and went about their business in spy-proof security.

Above, right and opposite: **The Boston Architectural Center, 320 Newbury Street.** The Boston Architectural Center is an architectural school and library, founded in 1889. Its present home, completed in 1967, is this six-story concrete building, located at the corner of Newbury and Hereford Streets. The building was designed by John Meyer and Robert Goodman of the firm of Ashley, Meyer & Associates, and displays on its Hereford Street side, especially, an intelligent sense of proportion through its rather heavily emphasized lines. On the opposite end of the building is a magnificent mural by artist Richard Haas *(opposite)*, depicting in its lucid trompe-l'oeil image an enormous palace of the Italian Renaissance.

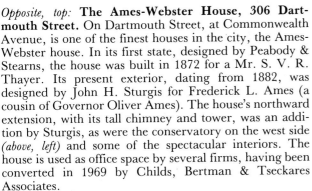

Opposite, top: **The Ames-Webster House, 306 Dartmouth Street.** On Dartmouth Street, at Commonwealth Avenue, is one of the finest houses in the city, the Ames-Webster house. In its first state, designed by Peabody & Stearns, the house was built in 1872 for a Mr. S. V. R. Thayer. Its present exterior, dating from 1882, was designed by John H. Sturgis for Frederick L. Ames (a cousin of Governor Oliver Ames). The house's northward extension, with its tall chimney and tower, was an addition by Sturgis, as were the conservatory on the west side *(above, left)* and some of the spectacular interiors. The house is used as office space by several firms, having been converted in 1969 by Childs, Bertman & Tseckares Associates.

Opposite, bottom: **The Boylston Street Fire Station, 953 Boylston Street. The Institute of Contemporary Art, 955 Boylston Street.** These two Romanesque-style buildings, erected in 1886–87, were designed by the architect Arthur H. Vinal (ca. 1854–1923). Their walls are made of a reddish-brown sandstone and brick, with green copper trimmings along the roof-lines and turrets. While the fire station building (to the right in the picture) has always functioned as a fire station, its neighbor to the left served as a police station until 1965, when the Boston Redevelopment Authority took charge of it. It was later leased to the I.C.A. on a long-term basis. The conversion of the police station to space for galleries, offices and a restaurant was done by Graham Gund in 1974–75. It is an impressive example of the "make-it-new" trend.

Above, right: **Harbridge House, 12 Arlington Street.** Harbridge House, overlooking the Public Garden at the corner of Arlington Street and Commonwealth Avenue, dates from 1861. It was one of the first houses of Back Bay, following the landfill of the bay's saltwater flats that had begun in 1857. The house was designed by Arthur Gilman, the architect of Arlington Street Church, in the French Academic style that was fashionable in Boston during the 1860s. The facade, of Nova Scotia sandstone, is a model of restraint and order, with its earnest symmetry and unostentatious detail. In 1893, the owner of the house, J. Montgomery Sears, acquired the adjoining house at 1 Commonwealth Avenue, and combined the two houses into one. Mr. Sears and his wife, Sarah Choate Sears, were patrons of the arts, with strong interests in music and painting. Paderewski played the piano at a performance in the Sears house; Sargent painted there the portraits of Mrs. Sears and her daughter Helen; and Edwin Austin Abbey was their guest during the time that he was painting his murals for the Boston Public Library. Among their other guests over the years were Admiral Dewey and Prince Henry of Prussia. After World War II, the house was used as a convent school, run by the Ursuline Religious Order. From 1967 to the present it has been occupied by Harbridge House, Inc., a research firm.

Opposite: **The Cushing-Endicott House, 163 Marl-borough Street.** Bainbridge Bunting, in *Houses of Boston's Back Bay* [1967], calls 163 Marlborough Street "perhaps the handsomest house in the whole Back Bay." Designed by the firm of Snell & Gregerson, it was built in 1871–73 for Thomas Forbes Cushing. The mansard roof and the elegantly framed windows, with their sandstone trim, are in the French Academic style, and have an evenness of expression that appears both flamboyant and self-effacing at the same time. The house was owned by the Endicott family from 1898 until 1958, when this photograph of the second floor octagonal study *(bottom)* was taken. In recent years the house was known as Garden Hall, and served as a residence for young women. Now it is used as office space by several firms. Around the corner are 326–328 Dartmouth Street, two houses that were designed also by Snell & Gregerson, and built in the same year.

Above: **The Robert Dawson Evans House, 17 Glouces-ter Street (corner of Commonwealth Avenue). Nos. 196–198 Marlborough Street (corner of Exeter Street).** Two rather romantic old houses, both dating from the year 1886, are at 17 Gloucester Street and 196–198 Marlborough Street. The first house *(bottom)*, an imposing mass of red brick and brownstone designed by the firm of Sturgis & Brigham, was for a while the home of Robert Dawson Evans. Evans was a self-made man who made a fortune from his copper and gold interests, and was also president of the American Rubber Company. His house is now an apartment building. Nos. 196–198 Marlbor-ough Street (with an entrance also at 16 Exeter Street), designed by W. Whitney Lewis for E. P. Bradbury, has an intriguing combination of Richardsonian and Queen Anne style features *(top)*. It now houses dentists' offices on the lower floors, and apartments on the upper floors.

Left: **The Charles A. Cummings House, 109 Newbury Street.** The house at the corner of Newbury and Clarendon Streets was built for, and designed by, the noted architect Charles A. Cummings (1833–1906). It dates from 1871, and displays some of the features that are also present in Cummings' New Old South Church of 1874–75: the polychromatic building materials, the emphasis on surface ornament and irregular, complicated massing. Since 1923 the house has been used for commercial purposes.

Above: **The Hollis H. Hunnewell House, 315 Dartmouth Street.** Several blocks away, at the corner of Dartmouth and Marlborough Streets, stands a similarly complicated house, built in 1870 for Hollis H. Hunnewell. It was designed by the firm of Sturgis & Brigham. Margaret Henderson Floyd has noted, in *Victorian Boston Today* [1975], that the Hunnewell house is "one of the earliest instances of exterior ceramic ornamentation on a building in Boston." It functions now as a clinic for children.

Above and right: **The International Institute, 287 Commonwealth Avenue. Loyola House, 297 Commonwealth Avenue. No. 303 Commonwealth Avenue.** These three houses are in the Classical style of architecture that was used in the Back Bay during the 1890s. The edifice at 287 Commonwealth Avenue *(right)*, was built in 1892 for Herbert M. Sears. It was designed by the firm of Rotch & Tilden with Italian Renaissance features. The facade, of white limestone, has a serene and chaste look that is very appealing. Between 1942 and 1964 the house was used as an apartment building, and since 1964 it has housed the International Institute, a social-service agency for foreign-born residents. No. 297 Commonwealth Avenue *(above)* has a similar style. Designed by Peabody & Stearns, it was built in 1899 for James Draper, a wealthy silk manufacturer, and has been used for the last two decades or so as a Jesuit monastery. No. 303 Commonwealth Avenue, next door, was designed by McKim, Mead and White, and was built in 1895 for G. A. Nickerson. With its fortresslike facade of a light gray granite, this house takes the austerity and restraint of the Classical style to an unusual extreme.

Above: **The John F. Andrew House, 32 Hereford Street.** At the corner of Hereford Street and Commonwealth Avenue is the John F. Andrew house, designed by Charles F. McKim of McKim, Mead and White. Andrew, a noted Massachusetts Congressman and reformer, built this house in 1883–84. It is very civilized-looking—modest but stately in its exterior design. The placid facade, with its light brown brick and limestone, presents an attractive compatibility of building materials. There are Italian Renaissance features: the Palladian window and portico, for example *(above, right)*. There is a clarity of expression in these features which is probably the most appealing aspect of this well-made building. The house is now occupied by an M.I.T. fraternity.

Opposite: **Chamberlayne Junior College, 128–130 Commonwealth Avenue.** These unusual houses, located between Clarendon and Dartmouth Streets, were designed by S. D. Kelley in 1882, and were somewhat remodeled, ca. 1905. Although the facades are simple and symmetrical in design, they are rather extravagant in detail, with their Baroque curves and ornamentation. The tall windows on the second floors of the houses, with their round-arched window-heads, seem to reach for an effect of height and grandeur, but the outlandish brackets at the cornice, the heavy balustrades and the obtrusiveness of the stone carvings have the cumulative effect of dragging the facade downward. The houses are a product of Beaux-Arts eclecticism; their design is a French import, dug up from an earlier century and, as Bainbridge Bunting notes in *Houses of Boston's Back Bay*, they "seem rather out of place on Commonwealth Avenue." In their present state, the houses, now combined into one building, serve as the Admissions Office of Chamberlayne Junior College.

The Albert C. Burrage House, 314 Commonwealth Avenue. Albert C. Burrage was a lawyer and financier with a wealth of interests in gas companies and copper mines. In 1899 he built this magnificent mansion on the southwest corner of Hereford Street and Commonwealth Avenue for himself and his family. This fantasy in limestone was designed by Charles E. Brigham, and was modeled, more or less, on the sixteenth-century Château de Chenonceaux in the Loire Valley of France. It is an ostentatious display of a man's wealth and ambition, with a facade that has tacked onto it the most elaborate of details, gargoyles and cherubs being the most conspicuous among them. The interior is decorated in an equally elaborate manner, with its gold-leaf ceilings and its marble staircase *(opposite)*. Since 1957, the house has been used by the Boston Evening Medical Center.

Details of Back Bay houses. The houses of Back Bay provide an endless supply of artful exterior decorations. Pictured are details of the Coolidge House, 21 Fairfield Street (1880; W. Whitney Lewis, architect), showing its terra-cotta sunflowers *(right)* and its eccentric fenestration *(above)*. There are also some quieter details: Louis Tiffany's mosaics and stained-glass windows *(opposite, bottom)*, decorating 395 Commonwealth Avenue (1899; A. J. Manning, architect), and the placid Classical entrance and Palladian window of 419 Commonwealth Avenue *(opposite, top)*, formerly 24 Charlesgate East (1891; Peabody & Stearns, architects).

Opposite, top: **The William Lindsey House, 225 Bay State Road.** This viny Tudor manor on Bay State Road at Granby Street was once called "the Castle." Designed by the firm of Chapman & Frazer, it was built in 1905 for William Lindsey, a wealthy entrepreneur. In Bainbridge Bunting's view, "there is a plausibility about this building," although it is "crowded with so many features that they compete with one another." Owned by Boston University, the house was used for a while as a residence for the president of the university, but is used now for social and ceremonial functions.

Opposite, bottom: **The Oliver Ames House, 355 Commonwealth Avenue.** Oliver Ames, governor of Massachusetts from 1887 to 1889, was also a wealthy financier, with interests in a variety of business enterprises, including railroads, banks and shovel manufacturing. The house that he built at the corner of Massachusetts and Commonwealth Avenues was used by the governor, his wife (Anna Coffin Ames) and their six children as a winter residence. Although H. H. Richardson had been selected as the architect, it was Carl Fehmer to whom the governor turned for the final design. (The Richardson design can be seen in Henry-Russell Hitchcock's *The Architecture of H. H. Richardson and His Times*, 1961.) The

house was completed in 1882, and was one of the grandest in Boston. It is an enormous brownstone mansion, modeled after the French châteaux of the sixteenth century. Of note on the facade are the carved stone panels that decorate the house between its first and second stories. For many years, the Ames House was occupied by the national Casket Company. Now it is undergoing renovation and is to be leased in the future for office space.

Above: **The Hatch Shell, Charles River Esplanade.** When Maria E. Hatch died in 1926, her will turned $300,000 over to the City of Boston, on the condition that the money be used for the creation of a park, playground or public work of some other kind that would serve as a memorial to Edward Hatch, her brother. The money was put to use in 1940 when it paid for the construction of the Hatch Shell on the Charles River Esplanade. The shell's seven concentric rings, of concrete and granite, were designed by Richard Shaw. This structure is used for the open-air concerts that are given every July by the Boston Pops Orchestra. These concerts were the dream of Arthur Fiedler, who conducted the orchestra here when the concerts began in 1929, and who continued to conduct for five decades thereafter.

Downtown

The history of Boston does not pass easily from memory, for on every block downtown there are reminders of the past in either historic buildings or historic sites. On Tremont Street, between Park and Beacon Streets, there is the Old Granary Burying-Ground (*above*) where the remains of our greatest ancestors lie—Boston's founders and defenders. Samuel Adams was buried here, as were John Hancock, Paul Revere, Peter Faneuil and Robert Treat Paine. A granite obelisk marking the tomb of the parents of Benjamin Franklin stands in the middle of the burial ground as its most conspicuous monument. It was erected in 1827, and was designed by Solomon Willard, who was also the architect of the Bunker Hill Monument in Charlestown. In the background of the

photograph stands the Boston Athenaeum, which has been watching over these hundreds of graves since 1847.

Opposite: **The Old City Hall, 41–45 School Street.** The Old City Hall was built upon the foundations of its predecessor, a building designed by Charles Bulfinch and erected in 1810. Originally the Suffolk County Courthouse, from 1841 to 1862 it served as the City Hall. Its inadequate size was the reason for its replacement by the present building, constructed in 1862–65. The architects of the new building were Gridley J. F. Bryant and Arthur Gilman. The design has been described as "uninhibited" in its use of the French Second Empire style—there is a generous amount of ornamentation, and a striking dis-

play of superimposed columns and pilasters, all on a gleaming facade of white Concord (N.H.) granite. The Committee on Public Buildings, which selected the design, commented on its style in their Report of June 19th 1862: "The style selected is one which grows naturally out of the character and requirements of the structure. It will at once be recognized . . . as the prevailing style of modern Europe, a style which the taste of the present Emperor of France, in particular, has so largely illustrated in most of the modern works of the French capital . . . . We believe that it will commend itself . . . as graceful and harmonious in proportion and detail, and . . . light and cheerful in its prevailing character . . . ." Within a few decades of its completion, the city govern-

ment offices had outgrown the City Hall, and an annex had to be built, but it was not until 1968, when the new City Hall was constructed, that the building on School Street was retired. Facing almost certain demolition, it was saved when a preservationist and developer named Roger Webb was able to come up with a development proposal that convinced the city authorities of the building's value. In 1970–72 the Old City Hall was renovated and converted by Anderson Notter Associates to space for offices, shops and a restaurant. It is run now by the Old City Hall Landmark Corporation, a non-profit organization that has been given a 99-year lease on the building. The view in the photograph is from the west, looking over the King's Chapel Burying Ground.

Opposite: **Park Street Church, corner of Tremont and Park Streets.** The Park Street Congregational Society was organized in 1809 as a bastion of resistance against the strong Unitarian movement of the time. Its meeting house was built in the same year on the corner of Tremont and Park Streets, overlooking the Common. This view is from the end of Hamilton Place, off Tremont Street. Henry James once wrote of the Park Street Church: "Its spire recalls Wren's bold London examples, like the comparatively thin echo of a far-away song; playing its part, however, for harmonious effect as perfectly as possible." The church was designed in the Georgian style by the English architect Peter Banner (fl. 1794–1828). Solomon Willard was the chief carpenter of the building; he also carved the capitals of the columns that decorate the successive tiers of the steeple. The church's outer brick walls were originally painted a pearly gray, which they remained until 1914, when the paint was removed. In 1838 the height of the walls was increased by about 12 feet so that the basement level of the building could be enlarged and made more useful. By the end of the century, after the church had gone through a period of decline and was in need of money, this basement level was rented out for commercial use. In 1902 a deal was negotiated to sell the building to a business syndicate that intended to demolish it and erect an office building, but the public protest over this sale was so loud that it fell through. In later decades, after something of a renaissance, the church was able to reclaim the basement level for its own use (1945–50), and to pay for occasional programs of restoration work.

Above, left: **Tremont Temple, 88 Tremont Street.** Tremont Temple is the meeting place and headquarters of the Tremont Temple Baptist Church, a society organized in 1838 by members of the Charles Street Baptist Church who felt that the organization's antislavery position was not strong enough. The present church building, on Tre-mont Street between School and Bromfield Streets, was built in 1894–96, and was one of the first steel-framed buildings in Boston. Its facade is unusual, and the following description of it is by George C. Lorimer, who was Pastor of the Church at the time of the building's dedication in 1896: "The exterior . . . is built of Berea light sandstone through the first two stories with heavy iron piers on each side, and the decorations are entirely made up of Christian symbolism, such as the vine, the crown, the cross, the pomegranate, and the dolphin. Above the second story . . . the exterior is treated in a manner recalling that of the Doge's Palace at Venice, the window finishing being white terra-cotta, while the mass of the surface is broken up with a diaper pattern of colored marbles. Above this, there is a row of dark columns supporting the roof and giving a finish to the entire facade . . . ." The architect was Clarence H. Blackall, of Blackall & Newton, who described the facade as a "mosaic," with its 10,000 terra-cotta blocks arranged in an intricate color-pattern. Blackall wrote also: "Tremont Temple shows a deliberate attempt to treat the front of a building exactly as one would treat a water-color."

Above, right: **The Parker House, 60 School Street.** The Parker House, established in 1855 by Harvey D. Parker, is the oldest continuously operating hotel in America. The original Parker House, which stood on this site, was a five-story marble-fronted building, designed in the elegant French Second Empire style. It was one of the great hotels of its time. Charles Dickens stayed here during his visit to Boston in 1867. In 1927, the entire hotel was rebuilt, its exterior being designed by Desmond & Lord. The Parker House declined in the twentieth century, but was saved from destruction in 1969, when it was sold to the Dunfey family. The new owners have renovated the interior, and are turning the hotel back on-to the road of success.

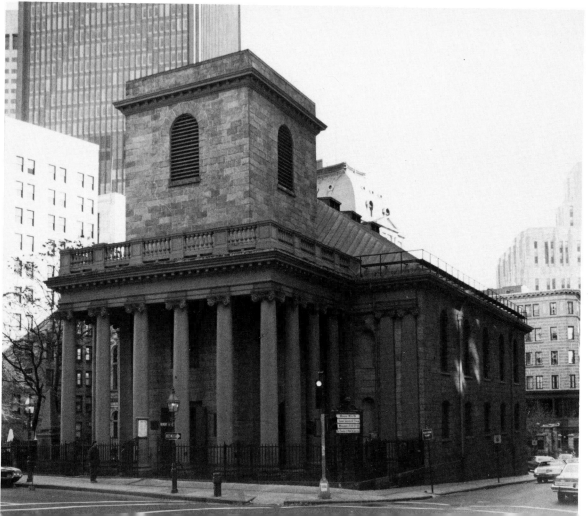

Opposite, top: **St. Paul's Cathedral, 138 Tremont Street.** The cornerstone of this Episcopal church was laid in 1819, and in the following year the building was consecrated as St. Paul's Church. In 1912 it was consecrated as a cathedral. Designed by Alexander Parris (also the architect of the Quincy Market Building), the structure was the first example in Boston of the Greek temple front. Its walls are of Quincy granite, and its Ionic columns and pediment are of Virginian sandstone. Solomon Willard, the architect of the Bunker Hill Monument in Charlestown, carved the capitals of these six columns. The stone in the tympanum remains uncarved, although a bas-relief of "Paul before Agrippa" was planned for it originally. The interior of the cathedral is richly decorated. The chancel was remodeled in 1913-27 by Cram & Ferguson.

Opposite, bottom: **King's Chapel, 58 Tremont Street.** The first Episcopal church in Boston was formed in 1686; its first building, erected in 1688, was a small wooden structure called King's Chapel. By the 1740s, this building was in a state of decay, and in 1747 a fund-raising drive was begun for the construction of a new building in stone. Construction began in 1749 and in 1754 the building was opened. It was designed by Peter Harrison (1716-1775) of Newport, and it is considered his best work. Fiske Kimball, in the *Dictionary of American Biography*, writes: "Harrison became the most notable architect of colonial America . . . . His buildings were exceptional in the America of that time for their purity of detail and their monumental qualities." The chapel was erected on the site of its predecessor, being built around the old building, which, on the completion of the new one, was dismantled and removed through the windows. Actually, the new building was never completed, for the elaborate steeple and

spire that Harrison's plan called for were never added on because of the expense they entailed. Harrison's plan was also compromised when the portico and balustrade were made of wood instead of stone, again for reasons of cost. These wooden details were made by Thomas Clement in 1785-87. The balustrade that he made originally ran along the top of all four sides of the building, but most of it was removed in the nineteenth century. The fortress-like walls of King's Chapel are of dark granite from Quincy and the building is notable for being the first major construction of cut stone in British America. The dark and gloomy exterior is more than compensated for by the richness of the interior, with its paired Corinthian columns along the nave and its fine decoration. King's Chapel today is Unitarian, having broken away from the Church of England in 1785. It was the first Unitarian church in the United States.

Above: **The Boston Young Men's Christian Union, 48 Boylston Street. The Hotel Touraine, 62 Boylston Street.** The Boston Y.M.C.U. is a recreational center for young men, founded in 1851. Its building on Boylston Street, between Tremont and Washington Streets, designed by the architects Nathaniel J. Bradlee and W. T. Winslow, was constructed in 1875-76. The Italian Gothic facade of the building has seen some better days, undoubtedly, but it is noteworthy still for its unusual details. It was enlarged at the rear in 1883, and again in 1912, but the most significant alteration was the removal of the tower that once stood atop the projecting pavilion on the facade's left side. To the right of the Y.M.C.U., at the corner of Boylston and Tremont Streets, stands the former Hotel Touraine, an elegant edifice built in 1897-98, and designed by the firm of Winslow & Wetherell.

Province Street. This little street, extending from Bromfield Street to School Street, was once the back alley that led to the rear grounds and stables of the Province House, a mansion that was used as the royal governor's residence during much of the colonial period. The Province House was a fine brick structure of three stories, built in 1679 by Peter Sargeant. It stood until 1864, when a fire burnt it down. The first view of Province Street *(opposite)*, looking north toward the Boston Company Building, presents an assortment of architectural styles in a typical Bostonian heap. The odd layout of the streets downtown has a way of producing this jumbled look, and is also responsible for the large number of peculiarly shaped buildings which have had to be built upon irregular lots. Looking south *(above)*, we see the dilapidated remains of Wesleyan Hall (center) at 36–38 Bromfield Street. Once the headquarters of the Methodist Church in Boston, the building dates from 1870, and was designed in the French Academic style by Hammatt Billings (1816–1874).

The Little Building, 100 Boylston Street (corner of Tremont Street). The Blake Building, 483 Washington Street (corner of Temple Place). These two buildings are examples of a very attractive style of architecture that was to develop, later on, into the Art Deco or Moderne style. There is an emphasis, in the design, on long vertical lines and on a Gothic angularity, along with a show of elaborately decorated surfaces. The Little Building *(opposite)* was designed by Clarence H. Blackall, and dates from 1916. The Blake Building *(above)*, by architect Arthur H. Bowditch, dates from 1910.

Above: **The Boston Post Building, 17 Milk Street.** The *Boston Post* was a popular Democratic newspaper, founded in 1831. It was well known for its humor and personal gossip, but was respected as well for its coverage of the political and financial worlds. The Boston Post Building stands on the site of the wooden house where Benjamin Franklin was born in 1706, and a bust of Franklin *(above, right)* decorates its facade in commemoration. The building dates from 1873–74, and its design has been attributed to the firm of Peabody & Stearns. Its cast-iron front displays a curious variety of Neo-Grec details.

Opposite: **The Transcript Building, 322–324 Washington Street.** The *Post*'s neighbor, on the corner of Milk and Washington Streets, is the Boston Evening Transcript Building. Founded in 1830, the *Transcript* was one of the city's greatest newspapers. Throughout its history of over 100 years, its dignified and highly literate pages earned it a devoted readership, most of which came from the conservative residents of Back Bay and Beacon Hill, generally, who were Independent Republican in politics. The Transcript Building, designed by Gridley J. F. Bryant & Louis Rogers, was completed in 1874. Its facade of Concord granite incorporates on the Washington Street side the remains of the facade of the earlier Transcript Building, which had burnt in the great fire of 1872. The mansard roof is iron-framed and iron-finished. The room inside this top story was the newspaper's composing room. The lower floors were offices, and in the basement were the press and folding machines.

Above: **The Old Corner Book Store, 285 Washington Street.** This building was constructed by Thomas Crease, an apothecary, in 1711 or 1712. Crease himself lived there until 1727, with his shop occupying the ground floor of the Washington Street side of the house. After a succession of owners during the next 100 years, the building was bought in 1828 by the bookselling firm of Carter & Hendee. The bookstore was made famous by the firm that took it over in 1833, William D. Ticknor & Co. (1833–45), later Ticknor & Fields (1845–65). Ticknor was Nathaniel Hawthorne's publisher and friend, Robert Browning's first American publisher, and the owner from 1859 to 1864 of the *Atlantic Monthly*. In these and many other capacities he contributed greatly to the literary life of Boston. The bookstore was run by several other firms (including E. P. Dutton & Co., 1865–69) after Ticknor & Fields left it. In 1903 it became a tobacconist's shop. It went through a period of neglect and decline, but in 1964–67 it was restored to its nineteenth-century state, and is now a classified advertising office of the *Boston Globe*.

Left: **The Boston Five Cents Savings Bank, 10 School Street.** Across from the Old Corner Book Store, on an odd pie-shaped lot, stands the new addition to the old Boston Five. Completed in 1972, it was designed by the firm of Kallmann & McKinnell, also the architects of the

new City Hall. The building's imaginative use of glass and concrete has earned it a place of distinction among contemporary works of architecture in Boston. The reflections of Washington Street that play on the surface of its broad curve of glass are not the least of the qualities that contribute to the Five's appeal.

Above and right: **The Winthrop Building, 7 Water Street.** The Winthrop Building (originally the Carter Building) stands on a narrow, oddly shaped lot between Washington and Devonshire Streets that was once a part of the large parcel of land along Washington Street owned by Governor John Winthrop, the first governor of the Massachusetts Bay Colony. This building was designed by Clarence H. Blackall, of the firm of Blackall & Newton, and dates from 1893–94. It has a very attractive entrance on Water Street *(right)* and a facade of yellow and orange brick and terra-cotta. It has also the distinction of being the first steel-framed building in Boston.

Opposite: **Old South Meeting House, 310 Washington Street.** The Third Church of Boston, a congregational society formed in 1669, was also known by the name South Church, and later, Old South Church. Its first meeting house, the Cedar Meeting House, was built in 1669 and stood until 1729, when it was torn down to make way for a new and larger structure. The present Old South Meeting House was built on the same site in 1729–30 by the masons Joshua Blanchard and Nathaniel Emmes. It was designed by an unidentified architect in a Georgian style similar to that of Christ Church, although the steeples of the two churches are rather different. The steeple of Old South has an unusual octagonal shape, and its spire is covered with copper. The interior of the building differs also from that of Christ Church. as it follows the meetinghouse plan, with the pulpit on the side, rather than on the end opposite the entrance. The Old South Church used the building until 1872, when it moved to a new building at Copley Square. The building was then leased to the U.S. government, which used it as a post office until 1876, when it was slated for demolition. But there was such a public outcry over this plan that demolition was called off, and a fund-raising drive to save the building was launched. The reason for the success of the drive lay in the place the Meeting House had earned itself in American history during the years before the Revolution. It was here that the meetings were held that led to the Boston Tea Party on December 16, 1773, and it

was here that many other town meetings were held, when Faneuil Hall proved unable to hold the large crowds. In 1775–76, when the town was occupied by the British, the Old South Meeting House's interior furnishings were stripped away by the British soldiers and used as firewood. Then the floor was spread with gravel, so that the building could be used as a riding school for the soldiers. It was not until 1782–83 that the building's interior was restored to its earlier appearance and use. After Old South was saved from demolition in 1876, it was taken over by the newly formed Old South Association, which in subsequent decades used the building as a lecture hall and historical museum. The association owns the building today, and runs it in cooperation with the National Park Service.

Above: **Filene's, 384–426 Washington Street.** This great department store was established in 1881 by William Filene in a small building on Water Street. In 1890, the store moved to Washington Street, and in 1912, the present building, at the corner of Washington and Summer Streets (an intersection known as "the Downtown Crossing," now a pedestrian mall), was built. It was designed by Daniel Burnham (1846–1912), and has a grand and dignified presence—conservative in style, yet offering an attractive measure of terra-cotta decoration. It stands in the heart of the busy Washington Street shopping district, and does much to set the mood of its environment.

Opera House (formerly The Savoy Theatre), 539 Washington Street. The Savoy Theatre, originally the B. F. Keith Memorial Theatre (or RKO Keith Memorial Theatre, as it was known after 1931 or so), was built upon the foundations of the old Boston Theatre of 1854. It was one of the great picture palaces of its time, but there were also live vaudeville acts on its stage: Al Jolson and George M. Cohan played the theater when it opened in 1928. The Keith became the Savoy in 1966, by which time it was used as a movie theater almost exclusively. The white terra-cotta facade on Washington Street *(above)*, designed by Thomas Lamb (1871–1942), looks like a Hollywood dream, with its imitation-Heaven ornaments and star-ward verticality. The interior of the theater *(opposite)* is even more extravagant, with its marble columns and gold decoration. The Washington Street theater district has slipped into decadence over the years, but there is a chance that it will revive in the 1980s. The Savoy Theatre, for example, was purchased in 1978 by the Opera Company of Boston and is now used as an opera house.

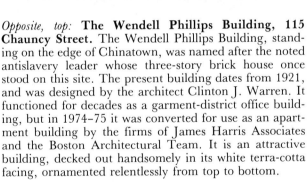

Opposite, top: **The Wendell Phillips Building, 115 Chauncy Street.** The Wendell Phillips Building, standing on the edge of Chinatown, was named after the noted antislavery leader whose three-story brick house once stood on this site. The present building dates from 1921, and was designed by the architect Clinton J. Warren. It functioned for decades as a garment-district office building, but in 1974–75 it was converted for use as an apartment building by the firms of James Harris Associates and the Boston Architectural Team. It is an attractive building, decked out handsomely in its white terra-cotta facing, ornamented relentlessly from top to bottom.

Opposite, bottom: **One Winthrop Square.** One Winthrop Square is one of the most successful examples of architectural renovation in downtown Boston. It dates from 1873, and was designed by the firm of Emerson & Fehmer. The facade posesses a banker's respectability, but has also enough character to appear familiar and appealing. It exhibits elements of the French Second Empire style in its elegantly framed windows, columns and projecting end pavilions, but there is also an Italian Renaissance influence. The light gray granite of the facade is from Hallowell, Maine. In 1973–74 decades of grime were removed from the granite surface, revealing its original brilliance of effect. The renovation work was by Childs, Bertman, Tseckares Associates, who converted it into a combination of shops and offices. Earlier occupants included its first occupant, the A. T. Stewart department store, and the *Record American* newspaper (1924–72).

Above, left: **The Church Green Block, 105–111 Summer Street.** This unhappy-looking building dates from 1873, and was designed by Jonathan Preston. It stands on the site of one of Charles Bulfinch's finest creations, the New South Church (built in 1814, demolished in 1868). Its location, at the joining of Bedford, Lincoln and Summer Streets, was once a lovely, tree-lined residential area. By the second half of the nineteenth century the area had become a commercial center, the heart of the city's shoe and leather trade. The Church Green Block was the headquarters, for a while, of the Shoe & Leather Exchange. It was later called the Regal Building when occupied by the Read & White clothing company. It is now, however, a deserted wreck, vacant in all but a few of its rooms. A sub shop and a deli occupy two street-level storefronts, and a palm-reader operates out of a first-floor office.

Above, right: **The Hayden Building, 681 Washington Street.** On the corner of LaGrange and Washington Streets, in the heart of the city's crime-ridden "Combat Zone," stands a rugged and stalwart structure that is known as the Hayden Building. It was designed by H. H. Richardson in 1875, and is the famed architect's only remaining commercial building in Boston. The walls are of Longmeadow sandstone: rough-hammered and chocolate-colored. Originally, the building was owned by the heirs of the architect's father-in-law, Dr. John C. Hayden. It was then occupied for decades by various men's furnishings stores. The present occupant is "The Scene," established ca. 1968.

Opposite, bottom left and right: **The Ames Building, One Court Street.** The Ames Building, built in 1889–91, was for several decades the tallest building in the city. It was designed by the firm of Shepley, Rutan & Coolidge, the successor of the firm of H. H. Richardson. On its facade of gray granite are some Richardson Romanesque features *(opposite, bottom right),* but the more dominant style apparent is that of the Italian Renaissance.

Above and opposite, top: **The International Trust Company Building, 45 Milk Street.** A similar combination of styles appears in the International Trust Company Building at the corner of Milk and Devonshire Streets. This fine edifice of Indiana limestone dates from 1892–93, and was designed by William G. Preston. Originally it was only about half of its present size ; the portion that extends along Devonshire Streets and half way up the block on Milk Street (up to and including the Milk Street entrance) is the earlier section. The rest of it was added in 1908.

Above: **The Shawmut Bank of Boston, One Federal Street.** The Shawmut Bank of Boston was designed by the Architects Collaborative, and was completed in 1975. Its form is rather boxy-looking and uninspired, but its surface is more interesting: a tan-colored facing of precast concrete that has a sort of rough, rawhide-like texture. The building consists of an undistinguished, skyscraping tower and the long, low-rise section that appears in this photograph. The view is of the cavernous stretch of Devonshire Street, between Milk and Franklin Streets, where the older buildings that line one side see their reflections on the opposite side in the Shawmut's long, racy windows.

Opposite, bottom: **The Chadwick Building and Chadwick Park, 172–184 High Street.** The Chadwick Lead Works (now the Chadwick Building) was built in 1887 on designs by the architect William G. Preston, also architect of the International Trust Company Building on Milk Street and the Hotel Vendome in the Back Bay district. For years the home of the Sager Electric Company, it was renovated in 1980 for use by the Boston Blue Print Company. Its facade is decorated with brownstone gargoyles and other creatures. Next door is a new restaurant, Chadwick Park, which occupies a nice-looking example of a Panel Brick-style building (to use Bainbridge Bunting's term). Part of this building's artfully fashioned brickwork can be seen in the photograph.

Opposite, top: **The Wigglesworth Building, 89–93 Franklin Street.** Here is another example of this kind of decorative brickwork—the Wigglesworth Building at 89–93 Franklin Street, which dates from 1873, and was designed by the architects Nathaniel J. Bradlee and W. T. Winslow.

The McCormack Post Office Building, Post Office Square. The New England Telephone Building, 185 Franklin Street. Two examples of the Art Deco style in Boston are the McCormack Post Office Building *(above, left and right)*, completed in 1931, and the New England Telephone Building *(opposite)*, completed in 1952. Both were designed by Cram & Ferguson, also the architects of the John Hancock Building. The Art Deco style has a streamlined look: made to appear as if rushing into the future. At the same time, it reverts to the past, bearing a resemblance to the Gothic in its skyward aspirations.

Above: **South Station, Dewey Square.** This enormous example of turn-of-the-century Classicism, located at the intersection of Atlantic Avenue and Summer Street, was designed by the firm of Shepley, Rutan & Coolidge and built in 1897–99. It was once the largest and busiest railroad station in America, but handles only a few trains now on a reduced number of tracks. Purchased in 1965 by the Boston Redevelopment Authority, following a long period of decline, it was scheduled for demolition in 1973 so that a hotel and parking garage could be built in its place. Although the wing of the building that faced Atlantic Avenue was, in fact, demolished, the rest of the building survived. It was sold in 1979 to the Massachusetts Bay Transportation Authority, which will renovate it for use as an "intermodal transportation facility," i.e., a railroad, subway and bus terminal, containing also a parking garage, restaurants and space for offices and shops. This New South Station should be ready for use in 1985.

Opposite: **Details of buildings.** These photographs are of unusual details, decorating otherwise unimportant buildings, which illustrate several aspects of Boston's character, if it can be said of an entire city that it possesses a certain character. The frowning stone heads on the front of 44 Kilby Street *(bottom)*, for example, are appropriately located in the financial district. The Salada Tea Building *(top, right)*, a ten-story limestone edifice at Berkeley and Stuart Streets, is noted for its great bronze doors. The panels, depicting scenes from the history of the Ceylonese tea trade, are the work of sculptor Henry Wilson, 1929. Finally, there is the "Liberty Tree" plaque *(top, left)* on the exterior of 630 Washington Street. It marks the site of the original Liberty Tree, where the Sons of Liberty, a pre-Revolutionary political group, held their meetings to denounce the British.

Opposite, top: **The Fiduciary Trust Building, 175 Federal Street.** The architectural styles of Modernism and Pop were for many years two mutually exclusive domains, in direct and hostile opposition to each other. In the 1970s, however, they began to merge and influence each other, producing as offspring the Post-Modern (or Funky Modern) style and a sort of genteel Pop. These photographs illustrate Post-Modernism in its use of eccentric and attention-getting forms and its concern for surface. The Fiduciary Trust Building, designed by the Architects Collaborative and completed in 1977, has the form of an irregular hexagon, with its upper stories cantilevered on all sides. Its facing is of dark gray concrete, with an exposed aggregate of black pebbles on its surface, reminding one a little of elephant hide.

Opposite, bottom: **The First National Bank of Boston, 100 Federal Street.** The First National Bank of Boston has an odd shape, too, with its middle stories cantilevered in "pregnant" fashion. Its surface is made of polished slabs of red Carnelian granite, which decorate the walls of all 37 stories. The building was designed by the firm of Campbell, Aldrich & Nulty, with Carl A.

Morse, Inc., as consultant. Completed in 1971, it serves as headquarters for New England's largest and most powerful bank.

Above: **The Federal Reserve Bank of Boston, 600 Atlantic Avenue.** The Federal Reserve System, the nation's central banking system and regulatory agency, was established by an Act of Congress in 1913. The New England branch of the Fed is located in Boston, and the present building at the corner of Atlantic Avenue and Summer Street is its new headquarters. Designed by Hugh Stubbins & Associates, it was built in 1972–77. Consisting of a 33-story tower and a four-story connecting building which wraps itself around the legs of the tower, the complex occupies a 5.7-acre site in the center of the up-and-coming neighborhood around South Station. The tower's odd washboard form and its Venetian blind sunshades are hard to digest at first sight, but they give the viewer something to chew on, and create a lasting silvery impression in the mind's eye. The burnished surface of white aluminum is especially impressive, outshining even its neighbor of white travertine, the Keystone Building.

Above: **The Keystone Building, 99 High Street (at Congress Street).** The Keystone Building is the national headquarters of Keystone Custodian Funds, Inc., a financial institution established in 1932. The building was designed by the firms of Pietro Belluschi and Emery Roth & Sons, and was completed in 1970. Dubbed "the beehive" by the photographer, it looks just that, with its rows of identical bow windows and its rounded corners. The cellular aspect of the windows is made even more apparent by the contrast of the bronze-tinted glass with the white facing of travertine marble. The building lacks any sharp edges in its overall design, and in this respect it represents a departure from the standards of severity and angularity that have governed corporate aesthetics in recent years.

Opposite, top: **The Bedford Building, 99 Bedford Street (corner of Lincoln Street).** On Bedford Street, in what was once the city's shoe and leather district, is the Bedford Building, an interesting specimen of the Ruskinian Gothic style. Built in 1875–76, it was designed by Cummings & Sears, also architects of the New Old South Church in the Back Bay. Its walls have the polychromatic aspect that is associated with the Ruskinian style, and are made of red granite from New Brunswick and white marble from Tuckahoe, New York.

Opposite, bottom: **The Proctor Building 100–106 Bedford Street (corner of Kingston Street).** Nearby is the Proctor Building, a fancy little Florentine palace that is home to a tobacco store and a restaurant. It was designed by the firm of Winslow & Wetherell, and dates from 1897.

The Old Court House, Pemberton Square. Suffolk County Court House Extension, Pemberton Square. The Leverett Saltonstall Building, 100 Cambridge Street. Center Plaza Building, Cambridge Street. At the foot of Beacon Hill stands a cluster of large buildings that is part of Boston's showy Government Center area. Behind the broad curve of Center Plaza *(opposite, bottom)*; (built in 1966–69 and designed by Walton Becket & Associates) are the Old Court House (1886–95; George A.

Clough); an enormous granite block designed in the German Renaissance style, and the Suffolk County Court House Extension (1937; Desmond & Lord), a rather mediocre specimen *(above).* The Extension competes, in its mediocrity, with the Leverett Saltonstall Building *(opposite, bottom;* Emery Roth & Sons), which stands to the right of the Extension and houses the offices of the Massachusetts state government.

Opposite: **City Hall, Cambridge Street.** Boston's Government Center, "one of the best urban spaces of the 20th century," according to Ada Louise Huxtable of the *New York Times* (September 11, 1972), occupies 60 acres of downtown land, and displays the new City Hall as its sparkling show-piece. Designed by the firm of Kallmann, McKinnell & Knowles, the building was completed in 1969. The interesting arrangement of its large concrete slabs has a way of wringing unusual metaphors out of the architectural critic. It can be the grand piano of contemporary architecture or also a three-dimensional crossword puzzle. It can be an enormous spider, walking on stilt-like legs, a space ship, a labyrinth or an Aztec temple. It is "a pinnacle defying all space and time," to H. D. Hodgkinson *(Proceedings of the Massachusetts Historial Society, 1972);* to Von Eckardt of the *Washington Post* it is "a building of more guts and conviction than any other government building in this country, save the U.S. Capitol itself" (February 12, 1969). To yet another observer, the prison etchings of Piranesi are called to mind. With its palace-like aspect and its intimidating hugeness, it can seem scandalous to the taxpayer, out of place in this "era of limits," but in the long run, it will probably be considered one of the city's greatest buildings. In the year 2000, it will still look contemporary.

Above: **Richards Building, 112–116 State Street.** This office building on State Street, opposite India Street and the Custom House, is one of the few remaining cast-iron buildings in Boston. Of the others, the McLauthlin Building at 120 Fulton Street, the Boston Post Building at 17 Milk Street and the building at 40–46 Summer Street are the most notable. Erected in 1867, the Richards Building was remodeled in 1889 after it was purchased by Calvin A. Richards, a wealthy merchant who made a fortune in the wholesale liquor trade during the 1860s. In 1874 he became a director of the Metropolitan Street Railway in Boston, and in 1885 he was made president of the American Street Railway Association. The Richards building looks much as it did late in the nineteenth century, except that the iron columns that once decorated the first and sixth levels have been removed.

Opposite: **The Boston Company Building, One Boston Place.** The Boston Company Building stands at the corner of Washington and State Streets. Owned by the Equitable Life Assurance Company of America, it is occupied by one of the city's major financial institutions, the Boston Company, Inc., and its subsidary, the Boston Safe Deposit and Trust Company. It was designed by Pietro Belluschi, along with Emery Roth & Sons. Ground was broken in 1967; construction was completed in 1970. The walls are made of bronze-tinted glass and aluminum. For structural suppport there are nine columns at the building's core, a long tapering column at each corner of the exterior, as well as the diagonal supports that are visible in this photograph. Viewed from the lower end of State Street, the Boston Company commands the attention of its neighbors, with its great height (41 stories or 605 feet) and dark imposing mass. State Street is said to have been a well-traveled Indian footpath in 1630, when the town of Boston was founded. The town's principal houses and public buildings were built around the square at the upper end of the street, and throughout the seventeenth and eighteenth centuries this area was the town's center of activity. The Boston Company Building is located on the site of the second meeting house, built in 1640, and of the Old Brick Meeting House, which was built in 1711 after a fire destroyed the earlier wooden building. The square was the location of the marketplace, and was also the site where public whippings and other punishments were meted out to violators of the town's strict religious laws. Situated in the middle of the square, and standing now in the long shadow of the Boston Company, is the Old State House. State Street, once called "the market street," was later named King Street (1708), before it was given its present name in 1788. By the late

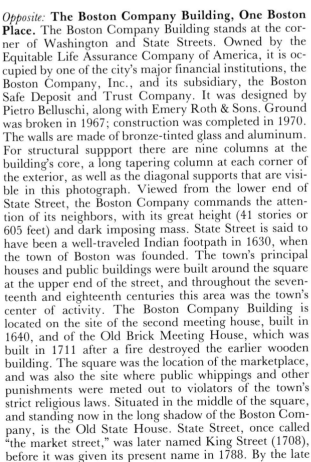

eighteenth century, State Street was lined on both sides with taverns, as well as with the town's largest commercial buildings. From the early part of the nineteenth century to the present, the street has been a financial center. The large building on the left in the photograph is the State Street Exchange Building, at 53 State Street, built in 1889–91 and designed by Peabody & Stearns. On the opposite side of the street is the India Building, at 84 State Street, also by Peabody & Stearns, built in 1904. It is now the home of the Northland Investment Corporation.

Above: **The Charles F. Hurley Employment Security Building, Cambridge Street. The Erich Lindemann Mental Health Center, Staniford Street at Merrimac Street.** The Hurley Building (completed in 1970; Shepley, Bulfinch, Richardson & Abbott, architects, with Paul Rudolph as associate architect) and the Lindemann Center (completed in 1971; Desmond & Lord, architects, with Paul Rudolph as associate architect) are two of the three buildings planned for the huge government complex called the State Service Center. The third building, a 33-story tower, has yet to be built, and perhaps never will be built, but there is little reason to be disappointed by this fact. Under Paul Rudolph's direction, the State Service Center's design became a monument to inutility and self-indulgence—a pointless muddle of forms expressing all the arrogance and brutality of government at its worst. "This thing has won awards, believe it or not," say employees of the Lindemann Center, and they explain also that the twisting, maze-like corridors inside the building are very confusing for their incoming patients. The exteriors of the Lindemann Center and of the Hurley Building are of hammered concrete, and resemble the barren lava fields around the sides of a volcano.

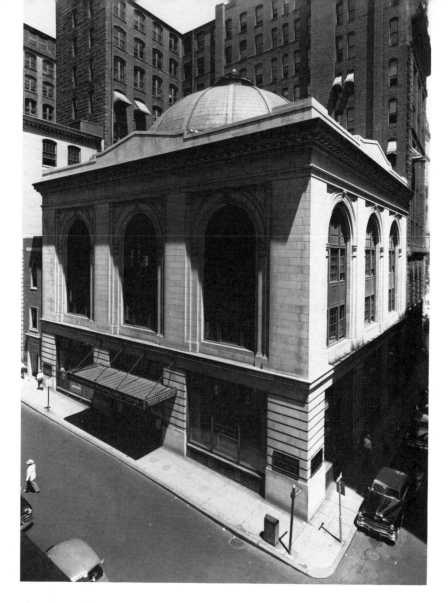

Above: **The Boston Stock Exchange, 30 Congress Street.** This building, designed by Peabody & Stearns and built in 1908, was for years the Boston Stock Exchange. Later, it was used by the Rockland-Atlas National Bank. Later still, until 1980, when it was demolished, it was the home of the Workingmen's Co-operative Bank.

Opposite: **The Old State House, 206 Washington Street.** The Old State House stands in the square near the intersection of Washington and State Streets. This square was Boston's first marketplace during the earliest years of the town's history. On this site in 1658 the first Town House, a wooden structure, was built. The building functioned as a merchants' exchange (first floor) and as the seat of colonial and town government (second and third floors). It was destroyed by a fire in 1711. The cornerstone for a second Town House was laid on the same site in 1712, and in 1713 the construction of this building was completed. The architect of the second Town House, or State House, as it was also called, is unidentified, but we know that the man who oversaw the building's construction was named William Payne. Designed in the English Renaissance style, it was considered one of the most elegant works of architecture in town. In 1747 a fire destroyed all but its outer brick walls, but in 1748 it was rebuilt to look much as it had. Although the present building has undergone much restoration and remodeling over the years, it retains some of the brickwork of 1712 and some of the original details and structural elements of the 1748 construction. The town government moved to Faneuil Hall in 1742, but the seat of colonial and state government remained in the Old State House through 1798, when the new State House on Beacon Hill, designed by Charles Bulfinch, was opened for use. In 1803, the state sold the Old State House to the town of Boston, which leased it for commercial use until 1830. In 1830 it underwent some remodeling by Isaiah Rogers, and from 1830 to 1841 it was used as the City Hall of Boston. From 1841 to 1881, when it was again leased out for commercial use, it suffered much neglect and deterioration — so much so that in 1876 it was threatened with demolition. A movement to preserve it succeeded, however, and during 1881–82 it underwent extensive restoration work under the supervision of George Clough, the City Architect. In 1903–04, a subway station was built underneath the Old State House, and its basement was used as the entrance to the station. Further restoration work was done during 1909–10 by Joseph Everett Chandler, who was commissioned to restore the building to its "provincial condition." The Old State House stands today in its preserved and restored state, and is cared for by the Bostonian Society, an antiquarian organization that has occupied the building and maintained its offices and a museum there since 1881.

DATE DUE

BRODART, CO.   Cat. No. 23-221-003